"Wish You Were Here"

ARKANSAS POSTCARD PAST

1900–1925

Dear Cleda:—
Sunday afternoon and I was just wondering if Cleda would attend the League and I hope she and the girls will all attend.
Give my best regards to all the League members.
I remain,
your friend,
Laura

Miss Cleda Paxton,
Harrison,
Ark.

"Wish You Were Here"

ARKANSAS POSTCARD PAST

1900–1925

Steven Hanley and Ray Hanley

THE UNIVERSITY OF ARKANSAS PRESS

FAYETTEVILLE • 1997

Copyright © 1997 by Steven Hanley and Ray Hanley

All rights reserved
Printed in Canada

01   00   99   98   97   5   4   3   2   1

Designed by Ellen Beeler

☉ The paper used in this publication meets the minimum requirements of the American National Standard for Permanence of Paper for Printed Library Materials Z39.48-1984.

Library of Congress Cataloging-in-Publication Data

Hanley, Steven G., 1952–
    Wish you were here : Arkansas postcard past, 1900–1925 / Steven Hanley and Ray Hanley.
      p.   cm.
    Includes bibliographical references and index.
    ISBN 1-55728-451-2 (pbk. : alk. paper)
     1. Arkansas—History—Pictorial works. 2. Postcards—Arkansas. I. Hanley, Ray, 1951–   . II. Title.
F412.H36   1997
976.7—DC20
                                                                     96-42245
                                                                           CIP

To our parents
Wallace R. Hanley, 1909–1974
Inez Hanley, 1921–1988

They were born during the era shown in this book, to parents who lived the Arkansas lifestyle pictured here. We know they both would have been very proud of the project, and we dedicate it to their memory.

To the next generation
Rachel Lydia Hanley, 1983–
Emily Jeanne Hanley, 1986–

The world in which they will grow up, have children, and earn their living will be increasingly different from that of the Arkansans pictured in this work. It is our hope that in the years to come they will turn to this book on occasion and renew their connection with the people, places, and values of an earlier time.

CONTENTS

Preface   ix

Introduction   1
Northwest Arkansas   11
North-Central Arkansas   69
Northeast Arkansas   107
Eastern Arkansas   155
Southeast Arkansas   185
Southwest Arkansas   231
Arkansas River Valley   299
Central Arkansas   345
Garland County and Hot Springs   411
Then and Now   455

Bibliography   471
Index   473

PREFACE

The cards that illustrate this work are a sampling taken from a collection of some five thousand pre-1925 Arkansas postcards that had its beginning in 1975 when the authors, on impulse, picked up a few at a local flea market. This began a combination of career and hobby: we found ourselves to be deltiologists, or collectors of postcards. The feature "Arkansas Postcard Past" began a daily run in the *Arkansas Gazette* in 1986, moving to the *Arkansas Democrat-Gazette* with the demise of the older newspaper in 1992. Over the years many readers of the feature wrote to say, "Have you done a book?" The completion of this work both responds to those faithful readers and fulfills one of our dreams.

INTRODUCTION

Wish you were here" was an often-penned phrase used in turn-of-the-century Arkansas on the back of postcards purchased for a few pennies and mailed with a one-cent stamp. From Little Rock and Hot Springs, from small remote places like Jasper in Newton County and Waldo in Columbia County, and from places now wiped off modern maps, like Mackinaw in Layfayette County, picture postcards were mailed by countless thousands. These views of everyday life—schools, main streets, churches, libraries, post offices, fires, and floods—all captured a view of early twentieth-century Arkansas that is recorded nowhere else. The purpose of this book is to share some of these views with present-day readers.

Arkansas was to share in the postcard craze with the rest of the nation and the world. The American infatuation had its genesis in 1893, when the first souvenir postcards were issued in conjunction with the World Colombian Exposition in Chicago. In 1898 federal law was changed to permit the sending of privately printed cards through the mail at a fee of one cent per card. As a result, interest in publishing, buying, and collecting the cards grew rapidly.

By 1906 postcards had become an established business in Arkansas, but most cards were printed in Europe, using photos taken in the larger Arkansas towns. The best quality cards were printed by German lithographers. The Germans were considered the world's masters of lithographic printing, a process wherein images on separate, specially prepared stones were used to print each color on the card. Most American cards were printed in Germany until 1909, when a U.S. tariff was imposed by Congress to protect the American printing industry. The following year one New York City firm employed six hundred people to produce postcards, and up to three million per day were printed.

As interesting as the surviving early twentieth-century postcards are today, it is also fascinating to explore the evolution of the postcard phenomenon. Although the first cards to generate mass interest originated in Europe, the craze quickly attracted the talents of American businessmen. This book shows samples of their products, remnants of the millions of postcards that were produced in the early years of this century.

The commercially printed cards were usually produced in large quantities; as a result, more of these have survived to be found by modern collectors. The original wholesale price for such cards, sometimes quoted on the back of the salesmen's samples, was a little as five dollars for a thousand cards. Current collector's prices for mass-produced cards that originally sold for a penny or two each, now range from a dollar to perhaps ten dollars apiece.

Professional photographers in communities across America quickly took advantage of the popularity of postcards. A professional's work would usually carry his name or his business's on the front of the card, sometimes with the date the picture was taken. Some of these cards, known in modern collector's parlance as "real photos," offer very sharp images taken with a professional's eye. These cards often portray small-town streets teeming with activity, as on market day or during a parade.

Local professional photographers sometimes used the "bird's-eye view" perspective in creating postcards of small-town America; these were usually taken from a water tower, rooftop, or nearby bluff. Such photographers also focused at times on the aftermath of fires, train wrecks, and natural disasters as subjects for the postcards they produced. These real photo cards have the greatest value to modern collectors; in mail auctions these often sell for one-hundred dollars or more.

Amateur photographers also developed an affinity for postcards, discovering the appeal of printing onto postcard stock their photos of family members, farm scenes, and simple everyday activities. Such photographers might print only one postcard of a favorite view, or perhaps create a dozen copies of a photo for mailing to family and friends. These bits of Americana often went through the photo albums of several generations before emerging into antique shops and estate sales. They are sold today at prices ranging from twenty-five cents to several dollars a card.

American interest in collecting postcards grew rapidly, following upon the popularity of these cards as a means to send a favorite view or short message. The volume of cards mailed offers evidence of the tremendous market from which collectors have drawn. Official United States Post Office figures for the year 1908 cite 667,777,978 postcards mailed in the nation; by 1913 this figure had risen to 968,000,000. This count was apparently reached by tracking the number of one-cent postcard stamps sold by the Postal Service. In a single day around Christmas in 1909, the St. Louis post office was noted to have handled 750,000 postcards, having a total weight of two and one-half tons.

One early commentary on the phenomenon of postcard collecting appeared in *American Magazine* in March of 1909 in an article entitled "Postal Carditis and Some Allied Manias." A portion of the essay states

> Postal carditis and allied collecting manias are working havoc among the inhabitants of the United States. The germs of these maladies, brought to this country in the baggage of tourists and immigrants, escaped quarantine regulations, and were propagated with amazing rapidity. A few of the pathogenic variety which had for decades been dormant have been by these foreign infections called again into activity and the result is a formidable epidemic. There is now no hamlet so remote which has not succumbed to the ravages of the microbe postale universelle. . . . Unless such manifestations are checked, millions of persons of now normal lives and irreproachable habits will become victims of faddy degeneration of the brain.

The postcard fad subsided after World War I, and interest in collecting cards declined but never died out completely. A revival in postcard collecting began in the 1970s, perhaps sparked by the nostalgia craze and a resulting increase in the market for paper collectibles. This revival has led to the creation of several publications specifically for postcard collectors, along with the institution of mail auctions for the sale of particular cards or groups of cards. Also common is the practice of sending postcard lots to collectors "on approval" so that cards may be selected for purchase. Hundred of full-time and part-time postcard dealers have emerged, traveling the United States to display their wares at postcard shows sponsored by local collectors clubs. All of these venues create a lively commerce in serving one of the most popular hobbies in the United States in the 1990s.

The postcard craze in America was at its height from 1900 to 1925, and cards of this era reflect a remarkable, rather remote period in the nation's and Arkansas's history. This period, sometimes referred to as "the good old days" by the grandparents of the baby boomers, covers a time before world wars were numbered, before the state's rivers were dammed, before most of our roads were paved, and when almost every small Arkansas town had passenger rail service. Everyday life was much more demanding in an era when illness and epidemics were common and antibiotics were thirty years in the future. For Arkansas workers, the hours were long, the pay was low, and benefits were nonexistent. The wife at home, often on a farm, ran her household without modern conveniences.

Despite the many hardships of Arkansas life in the first two decades of the twentieth century, this distant era has a certain appealing quality. Nowhere is its likeness better captured than on the picture postcards of the day. The images that were preserved on the front of the cards by the photographers were sometimes produced by commercial printers in large quantities but other times by small local photographers a handful at a time.

The historical value of these cards lies not solely in the photo, but often also in the messages that were mailed to friends or family. Economic hardships were reflected in some of the cards' messages, and they illustrate how hard people worked for what today seems so little money. Consider the following note from the tiny Clay County town of Moark in 1907: "I hope you have got done harvesting and thrashing by this time. I have been working in a sawmill but things are looking blue because they are talking of shutting down the mill as happened to all the other sawmills in the South." In this era there was no government assistance, such as unemployment benefits or food stamps, to fall back upon in such situations. A message from Marshall in 1912 reads, "Work has opened up here pretty good but wages are low and hours are long. I am working ten hours for $3.00."

Then, as now, not everybody was thrilled with their job, as in this example from Camden in 1910: "Hi Scrapper, I'm working too, am assistant stenographer and general flunky for a lumber broker." Sometimes a message reminds us just how much more a small job was valued than it is now, as in these 1910 words from Judsonia: "I just landed a good job for the summer picking berries. I will be paid two cents per quart, and that means if I can pick fifty quarts I will earn a dollar a day."

Education often found its way onto turn-of-the-century postcards, both in the photos of schools and students and in the messages. In 1910 the average Arkansas schoolteacher's annual salary was $273, and the state had an astounding 5,110 school districts. The teachers employed in these far-flung districts must have been truly dedicated in the face of frequent inconvenience and discomfort: a Little Rock teacher penned in 1910, "Just got back from the County Teachers' Association and we drove in carriages through the rain all the way. I just ruined my new suit."

Health care is a dominant topic as we near the close of the twentieth century, and it is also prevalent in early twentieth-century postcards. With few exceptions, only the larger Arkansas cities had hospitals; these were all featured on postcards. When illness struck Arkansas families eighty-odd years ago, tales of many long-since eradicated health threats were scrawled across the backs of postcards: from Rector, in northeast Arkansas, in 1911, "The smallpox are all over town and we are afraid we will get them." One can feel for the Van Buren woman who wrote in 1913, "I am just able to sit up and have been sick in bed five weeks with typhoid fever, all but three of us had it."

In this era before the invention of antibiotic medicines, common infections were sometimes deadly, and often the state's climate got the blame. A visitor to Little Rock in 1910 wrote home, "The climate in Arkansas is very bad. There's a lot of puddles of stagnant water with malaria all over them. There's more chills, fever and malaria than I ever heard of before." A message from the White County town of Higginson reported, "We are here and both sick, this shure is the land of the dog." A message from the Benton County community of Hiwasse in 1910 was, "I am way down in the Jungles of Arkansas."

A Missouri visitor to Yellville in 1913 sent home a card of the Marion County Courthouse with a hog rooting on the lawn and wrote, "Well I am in Arkansas. Somethings look very primitive, we are right on top of the mountains. Cedars are thick, hogs run every place, see lots of rail fences and log cabins."

The adage "When it rains, it pours" aptly describes the situation of an El Dorado woman in 1911: "Know you wonder why you don't hear from me but child my hands are too full to write. Amos had a spell of tonsillitis, Elizabeth has the measles, and Henry has been in bed for a week with neuralgia. Please write and tell me all the news and especially about the infantile paralysis." As great as her problems sound, a 1908 message from Van Buren surely reflected a family's even greater pain: "Little Dewey Pew died Thursday evening at 7:30 p.m. and was buried Friday, it was so sad." Then there were the simple words from a Hope woman in 1908: "rheumatism no better."

Accidents afflicted Arkansans then as now, and such was the case in 1910 in a note from a soldier at Camp Pike (today's Camp Robinson near North Little Rock): "Excuse me for not writing sooner but I've had a bit of an accident. I am athletic instructor here at the post and went to show some fellows how to do a horizontal bar stunt. The bar broke and put me on the blink." Yet another man in 1907 penned from Little Rock, "Just got out of a bad wreck without a scratch." A reader of the card some ninety years later must wonder what kind of vehicle was wrecked; it was most likely a wagon, although an early automobile is a possibility.

Some messages leave the present-day reader wishing for more details: "It seems strange to me that you didn't break your neck when you jumped out that window. What if you had been caught?"

In this day of satellite communications and cable television, news of natural disasters race around the globe in seconds. In turn-of-the-century Arkansas, postcards often carried the only photos of flood, tornado, and fire destruction. Even in less severe circumstances, commentary about the weather was often shared, as in this note from Fort Smith referring to a drought in 1909: "In some towns near here drinking water is at a premium, no rain for three months." Another Fort Smith writer gave thanks on his postcard in 1910: "So the comet [Halley's] passed and we are still here."

Postcards were also a medium for romance and rejection, some of which surely must have caught the postman's eye; a reading many decades later suggests that some aspects of human nature have changed very little. From Helena in 1908 came simply the words, "Sorry, but I am engaged to another." An apparently turbulent relationship in 1908 Jonesboro caused a man to confide by postcard to "Hazel," "Well, Eve and me quit last night and I guess it is for good this time cause I will never ask her for another date. I don't know her real reasons but I guess she knows her business, hope she is satisfied." The painfully rejected suitor continued his scrawled message across the front of the postcard view of the Jonesboro Methodist Church, "Eve may change her mind again. If she does she knows where to find me eighteen hours out of the day. Don't tell her that I told you so much but I don't care for her knowing I told you we had a fight." Fortunately for us later generations, not all Arkansas romances ended in failure. In 1912 a happy Pine Bluff lady wrote, "You will forgive me when I tell you all my spare time has been taken up in landing me a big Arkansas man. I am now Mrs. William Rice Kirby." From Berryville in 1910 came the message, "Reckon you are not married, I am expecting to hear of you eloping with some little lassie. Marrying seems to be the very latest style around here."

Some sweethearts couldn't have dreamed their poignant messages would appear in print almost five generations later, as in the case of a Fayetteville man in 1910: "Dear Anna, I'm so lonely for you, heartsick just for one sight of you. I'm starving for a glimpse of eyes so true. Dark are the nights the world seems, life holds no crave for pleasures gay, your sweet face haunts me day by day. Kiss to you XXX, Good-By-Dear."

As eloquent as Anna's sweetheart was, he paled in comparison to a romantic soul writing these words from Little Rock in 1912: "Mary Dear, when I come back to you there will be sweet birds calling, when I come back again songs of deep joy awaking after the storms and rain, there will be sunlight, skies will be shiny and blue when I am by your side, dear."

Some postcard commentaries on relationships were not what one would expect, especially since postmen and others could have read the cards. Such is the case on a postcard sent in 1909 by Diane of Conway to May, a student at Ouachita Baptist College in Arkadelphia, "Tell Vera I'm sleeping with Louis. Why didn't you come down to kiss Mich good bye?" Perhaps Diane's terminology carried a different connotation then than it does today.

All postcard messages were not reflections of happiness; many carried hints of loneliness and pleas for a letter or a visit. From Arkadelphia in 1907 came, "I don't care whether you have a good Christmas or not, for I know I shall not. I am here all alone and also by myself." A plea for contact came from a Batesville man in 1910: "How are you?

You must be dead, I haven't heard a word from anybody, I'm forgotten. I am lonely here kid, if you are not dead would be greatly pleased to see or hear from you. Now write or I will never write again, your loving friend."

On a happier note were the words written on the address portion of a postcard sent from Little Rock in 1910: "Oh carry me at a rolling rate to Jonesboro P.O. (in Arkansas land) and there in quiet let me be until Miss Kitty Decker comes to call for me." A 1908 message from Benton to a female student at Henderson College at Arkadelphia offered some hints about campus life, "We guarantee a good time or pay the freight both ways."

Institutions that are today either obsolete or tactfully renamed were subjects of many postcards, and often inspired interesting comments. From Little Rock in 1910, on the back of a card of the Arkansas Insane Asylum the message was, "What do you think of this hotel? I tried to get a room here but they wouldn't have me!" Penned on the back of a card of the St. Joseph's Orphanage in Pulaski County was, "I think I will have to go to this place and get me a little girl to raise, to be my sweetheart when she grows up. Ha Ha! There's some awful pretty kids in this place."

Politics were sometimes the subject matter of postcard messages, offering a unique view of the common man's perception of the current events of the day in Arkansas: from Gravette in 1912, "I have a five hour layover and Jeff Davis (Governor of Arkansas) is going to talk after dinner, guess I'll go to pass the time." From 1910 in Eureka Springs was, "I went to hear Carrie Nation speak last night and had a great time." The famous hatchet-wielding temperance crusader lived in the Carroll County resort for a time.

A Texarkana resident named Cyrill reported in 1909, "President Taft passed through here last Sunday. Papa stated there was 20,000 people there to see and hear him. The President was so hoarse he could not talk much. It was such a jam in the crowd that several ladies fainted and Papa said he almost fainted from the heat himself it was so suffocating. One woman cried and screamed like a child." By way of a historical footnote,

President William Taft would have been a formidable sight that hot summer day in Texarkana, as the commander in chief is said to have weighed approximately three hundred pounds, so large in fact that, on one occasion, he became stuck in a White House bathtub. The heat and crowds of the Miller County visit may well have distressed him also on that day in 1909.

As they are today, religion and church events were part of the fabric of Arkansas life in turn-of-the-century communities. Many cards were printed with views of churches ranging from the cathedrals in Little Rock and Fort Smith to the modest frame structures in small farming communities. From Brinkley in 1909 was written, "Rev. Hicks will be with you the 8th for a 3 week revival and he is under strict rules of diet. He will esteem it a great favor if you can have a pitcher of fresh buttermilk where he can use it instead of water. He will gladly reimburse any expense." A simpler message came from the heart of a small Dallas County child in Fordyce in 1908: "This is where I go to Sunday School, I have a little red chair to sit in. They give me a Jesus card every Sunday, do you get Jesus cards too, Grandma?"

Despite often grueling workdays, sports were one of the pastimes of Arkansans of the era, as illustrated in this message from Arkadelphia in 1909: "Had a football game yesterday with Centenary College from Shreveport, won score 83 to 0." Then there is what might be regarded as a prophetic comment from 1909, "I am writing this card on the front porch of the Hotel Astor at Benton, Arkansas, and just as I looked up I saw three hogs promenading on the hotel lawn. Evidently this is a great country for hogs."

The images that follow depict an Arkansas separated from ours by two world wars, a major economic depression, space exploration, and almost incomprehensible technological progress. Yet the words taken from the backs of these postcards suggest that, in the hearts and minds of Arkansans, the changes are perhaps not nearly so great as they seem at first glance.

NORTHWEST ARKANSAS

Benton, Boone, Carroll, Madison, Newton, and Washington Counties

The northwest corner of Arkansas is the heart of the Ozark Mountains and today is served by Highway 71, which was not built until 1930. By the dawn of the twentieth century, however, rail service had reached most of the small Ozark hamlets, and tourism would soon begin to contribute to a diversifying economy.

The greatest number of postcards of the region came from Eureka Springs, which came into its own as a nationally known resort with fine hotels, springs, and scenic views.

In Washington and Benton Counties, the population centers of the region, popular postcard subjects were the University of Arkansas, and the business districts of Fayetteville, Bentonville, Rogers, and Springdale. Tourism-related card subjects included the small resort towns of Sulphur Springs and Siloam Springs and, perhaps the most historically significant, the Monte Ne resort erected near Rogers by the eccentric entrepreneur Coin Harvey. Today most of the dream project of the erstwhile presidential candidate lies below the clear blue waters of Beaver Lake.

The fruit production of Benton and Washington Counties, in a time when the region led the nation in apple growing, is reflected on many postcards. The cards' views range from the fruit being picked in the orchard to its being packed in barrels for nationwide shipment or being made into vinegar in local factories. In point of fact it was agriculture that rebuilt Washington County, which had been severely damaged during the Civil War. In 1900 Washington County was home to 34,000 people, 43,000 pigs, 20,000 cows, and 7,000 sheep and produced 2,000,000 bushels of corn and 615,000 bushels of apples. Much of this activity, which would build the economy into what would someday be the state's strongest, was captured on postcards that surely stimulated further investment in the region.

While the railroad brought attention to towns like Harrison and Berryville, the lack of roads isolated some areas. The Madison County town of St. Paul and Newton County's Jasper all produced abundant hardwood lumber and barrel staves but lacked the refinements of schools and sidewalks that were captured on postcards of other communities of the region. The barrel-stave industry is long gone from the American scene, but in the early years of the century, Ozark hamlets built and shipped barrels of formed hardwood staves worldwide. Prohibition removed the American demand for whiskey barrels and precipitated the decline of the industry.

Northwest Arkansas of the late twentieth century has perhaps changed more, in terms of population and economy, than any other region of the state, and this change is apparent in the images of the region in this chapter.

Washington County was formed in 1828, with centrally located Fayetteville chosen as the county seat. The courthouse, captured in the reflection of a 1907 puddle, was constructed in 1904 and still serves the rapidly growing county today.

The town square, with the 1910 post office at its center (to the right), was for many years the heart of the city's business district, and even today remains a source of pride after its restoration. The raised crosswalk in the foreground helped strollers cross the often muddy, horse-worn street without soiling their shoes.

"Your Uncle Will has been very sick. . . . Mabel D. is very sick too think she has scarlet fever," is the 1908 message written on the back of a view of the historic Old Main building, the oldest and best-known landmark on the University of Arkansas campus. Requiring two years to construct with 260,000 pounds of iron and accented with gray limestone, the building dates from the 1870s.

College dorm life may have changed over the decades, but what appears to have been a dorm room is well-adorned with the pennants that have been a part of college life for years. Although not postmarked, this ca. 1910 card is most likely from the University of Arkansas in Fayetteville. One of the pennants is for Galloway, a women's college in Searcy, which may explain the photos of young women sprinkled among the pennants.

3482 Arkansas Building. Fayetteville, Ark.

Constructed in St. Louis for the 1904 World's Fair, the Arkansas Building was erected at a cost of nineteen thousand dollars. The building was the scene of a number of receptions and provided an opportunity to show off Arkansas to thousands of fairgoers. When the fair ended, Fayetteville resident Artemus Wolf bought the building with a bid of seventeen hundred dollars, disassembled it, numbered all the pieces, and shipped them back to Fayetteville, where the building was reassembled to serve as his home for years. Time and neglect took their toll, and the home was demolished in 1939.

"I am here at the station ready to start home in an hour. Have walked around to see quite a lot of Fayetteville this morning," reads a 1913 message on the back of a card of the Ozark Opera House. Erected by the Knights of Pythias in 1905 at a cost of twenty-five thousand dollars, the theater hosted a variety of vaudeville acts and motion pictures over the years. Today the building stands in boarded decay, its future much in doubt.

Among Fayetteville's handsome houses of worship was the domed First Baptist Church, erected in 1908 at the corner of Dickson and College Avenues. The building's dome developed stress fractures, which were a factor in its demolition in the 1950s.

Fayetteville had no hospital until after the turn of the century; surgery was generally provided in the local doctors' offices. The city's first hospital, depicted on this postcard, was dedicated in 1907. Insufficient funds and a lack of equipment delayed service to the first patient until 1912, the year this card was mailed.

Fayetteville, ca. 1910. Two well-dressed boys pose on a homemade cart in front of 113 West Lafayette Avenue. A. M. Byrnes, a contractor who had helped construct University of Arkansas's Old Main, built this house using lumber left over from that job. He built two more houses on the same plan for his two young daughters; he rented out the houses until his daughters were grown. The house in this view still stands.

The Washington County town of Shiloh was renamed Springdale in 1872, and the town grew rapidly in the shadow of adjacent Fayetteville. This ca. 1905 view was likely photographed from a telegraph pole, the wires of which are visible. Johnson's Dry Goods Store was having a big sale, which seemed to have attracted a long line of well-dressed ladies.

"I am in Springdale Ark. and can say this is a true picture. Fruit out here galore," was the 1911 message to Kansas. Most of the fruit from this orchard would have been shipped across the nation, although some would supply the canneries and evaporators that served the area.

"This is the picture of the Cannon ball wreck it did not hurt any one very bad," was the 1912 message sent from Springdale to Indiana. Trains were the dominant form of transportation in Arkansas at the time, and while wrecks were not uncommon, they always drew a crowd.

Among the many smaller towns dotting Washington County was the village of Lincoln. The frame building to the left, which no longer stands, offered meals for twenty-five cents. The building to the right, still standing today, was J. M. Smith's furniture and hardware store, a common small-town combination. The store also bears a prominent sign featuring Vulcan plows, which were essential in working the rocky Ozark soil.

Arkansas children have always found a dip in a creek to be an almost irresistible lure. These two girls near the small village of Cincinnati were photographed around 1910, complete with their bathing caps, swimming in the brush-choked creek.

The 1905 message mailed to what was then Indian Territory, now Oklahoma, reads, "Robbert how are you and the Indians getting along? Harrell has your horses run off with you yet?" The photo was taken near the Washington County community of Summers and shows a typical small sawmill operation with a portable steam engine powering the saws.

The completion of the Frisco Railroad's tunnel through the crest of the Ozarks in 1882 helped create the resort village of Winslow, which was named for the president of the railroad. "How do you like the teams they use in this country. Am enjoying my honeymoon in the Ozarks of Arkansas," comments the 1916 message on the back of this card showing a ox-drawn wagon.

"We were late 5 hours last night so lay over here. . . ." The thoughts of the purchaser of this Prairie Grove card of a cliff-side dwelling can only be imagined some eighty years later.

"I am sending a view of the train . . . depot at Elkins July 3, 09. Elkins is the next station to Harris." The card documents the fact that even the tiny Washington County towns of Elkins and Harris had rail depots, which were essential before the creation of decent roads and the coming of automobiles to the Ozarks.

"Just think if you could see me in Goshen," is the message from Washington County in 1914. Such comic cards, imprinted with a town's name, were popular in the early years of the century; romance was among the most common topics on such cards.

In the years before the state and federal governments created and funded welfare programs, the county poor farm was a fixture of Arkansas life. This surprisingly handsome brick structure would have been the last refuge for down-and-out families in Benton County.

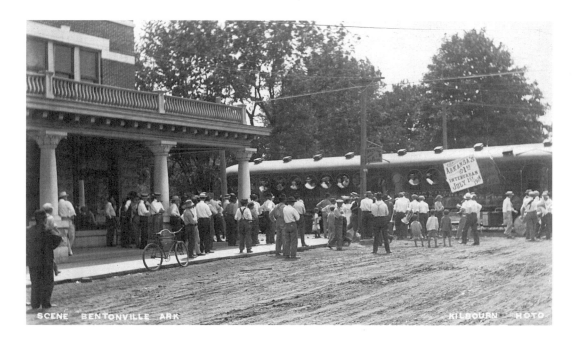

Bentonville, July 1, 1914. It was a banner day in front of the Massey Hotel when interurban railcar service was opened between the Benton County seat and Rogers, site of the main Frisco depot. The roundtrip fare on the ninety-two-foot-long red coach that seated 130 persons was forty cents. It would go out of business two years later, in part because of the competition of an increasing number of automobiles.

Gentry's Elberta Hotel provided room and board for visitors to the small Benton County town. Anyone sitting on the porch on the day in 1905 that this photograph was taken would have remarked upon the cap-adorned boys driving a cart pulled by two cows.

From Gentry around 1915 came the following message: "After living here a while, the life is not so simple, as you see these are not ox teams nor wagons. The fare is not so bad as you will observe the lady in white, who is crossing the street, she is not especially *thin*. I make haste to say that it is *not me*."

The coming of the Frisco Railroad in 1881 gave birth to the town of Rogers, which was named for Capt. C. W. Rogers, the general manager of the railroad. The 1912 card of a busy Saturday bears the words, "Arrived this after noon, the train was 3 hours late. The goods has not come yet."

Automobiles were beginning to show up on Arkansas's few roads, but as seen in this 1914 card, mules and horses still played a prominent role in the economy of northwest Arkansas.

"Dear Son This big train turned over and killed the fireman also engineer," are the words from the Benton County town of Lowell in 1912. Rail lines criss-crossed northwest Arkansas, helping the area prosper, but not without cost, as seen on this card mailed to Huntsville, Arkansas.

A thriving apple business and the railroad were the heart of the economy in tiny Centerton. The Benton County town's high school was built at a cost of only five thousand dollars, according to the message penciled on the back of this card printed around 1905.

Maysville is one of the oldest towns in Benton County, dating its start from 1839 on what was then a military road. This photo of the rough dirt Main Street was taken around 1900; today the buildings are all gone.

Before roads and automobiles, even the smallest Arkansas villages often had a well-stocked general store. Such was the case in tiny Yocum, located in Benton County. The man in the center, whose head was blurred because he moved as the camera shutter was snapped, is standing next to a large case of Post Toasties cereal.

Perhaps the most photographed store in northwest Arkansas was the "Arkansaw Store," its claim to fame being the distinctive sign on the front of the general store. The message sent to Maryland asks, "Have you any stores in Frederick as good as this one?"

CAVE AND SPRING AT CAVE SPRINGS, ARK.

Cave Springs was reportedly first named Cannon but changed its name around 1903 to match its best known landmark, the spring seen here gushing from a small cave.

The small Benton County town of Cave Springs was home to McDaniel's Livery and Feed. Coming down the center of the dirt street is what appears to be a pair of chickens. The town would prosper from the railroad and the apple trade, though both of these were gone by 1920, and Bentonville and Rogers would become the dominant towns in that part of northwest Arkansas.

3258 Old Eagle Hotel built in 1841 Siegel's Headquarters March 1861 Bentonville, Ark.

The Civil War played out across Benton County, and landmarks from the conflict often showed up on postcards. This ca. 1905 card's message is, "While Siegel [a Union general] was eating breakfast at this hotel, he was surprised by the Confederates and had to leave his meal unfinished. In 1895 he came back and said he came to finish his breakfast. He was an honored guest of both sides. The friendliness of the Confederates was somewhat of a surprise to him."

Known as the Kilhburg Hotel upon its opening in 1909, this Sulphur Springs resort hotel was thought to be the largest in northwest Arkansas at the time. By the time of this 1923 card, it had been renamed the Mountain View Hotel. Today only the bottom floor remains, and it is on the property of John Brown University.

The scenic Illinois River attracted sportsmen and photographers as it flowed through western Benton County into Oklahoma. Today the stream remains free-flowing and is a popular stream for canoeing.

Siloam Springs, originally named Hico, was said to have had twenty-seven springs; the largest of these was in the park where this large crowd spent a Sunday afternoon around 1910. This scene in the park, with its gazebo sheltering a band, is typical of small-town-America Sunday afternoons of the era.

Siloam Springs, ca. 1900. Grocer Ed McCulloch, in center with bow tie, posed in front of his store with a load of stock that was being delivered from the train depot by L. D. Leflar, who had a drayman's (delivery) service for fifty years. The smaller wagon to the right is the grocer's delivery wagon. [Card courtesy of Robert A. Leflar Sr. of Fayetteville, son of drayman L. D. Leflar on this card.]

An eccentric financier, William Coin Harvey came to the Ozarks and bought 320 acres six miles from Rogers. The resort of Monte Ne was created in 1901 when the first hotel opened. The rail station in the background of this view provided a rail link to Lowell, and presidential candidate William Jennings Bryan was the speaker on the depot's opening day. The gondolas transported visitors from the depot along canals to their hotels.

The Monte Ne resort hosted thousands of visitors during the two decades it operated. Among the attractions was this spring-fed, partially enclosed pool complete with diving platform. The men's bathing suits, in the style of the time, always included a shirt top.

Coin Harvey planned to construct up to six hotels at his Monte Ne resort, though only two were actually built. The Oklahoma Row, seen here around 1908, was constructed of logs and was three hundred feet long. In the distance to the left is the Bank of Monte Ne. The resort would fail by 1920, Harvey would die in the 1930s after losing badly as the Liberty Party candidate for U.S. president in 1932, and finally the rising waters of Beaver Lake would inundate the remnants of Monte Ne in the 1960s.

The Carroll County town of Green Forest had in its town square a small park, elevated above the dusty street. Townspeople and park visitors would ride their horses and drive their buggies and wagons into town, where they would tether the animals to the rail that encircled the park. This card was mailed to Indiana in 1914.

"Oh! but we will have fine times when you come," is scrawled on the back of a card of the brick school building in the town of Green Forest. The state's first mandatory school-attendance law might have been on the minds of the students here; it had just been enacted in 1909, the year before this card was mailed.

Berryville was laid out in 1850 and named for James H. Berry, who had established the first store in eastern Carroll County. Largely destroyed during the Civil War, Berryville grew rapidly during the first two decades of the twentieth century. The coming of rail service helped support a thriving business district around the town square; this 1905 view is of the east side of the square. Today the buildings still stand but contain other businesses.

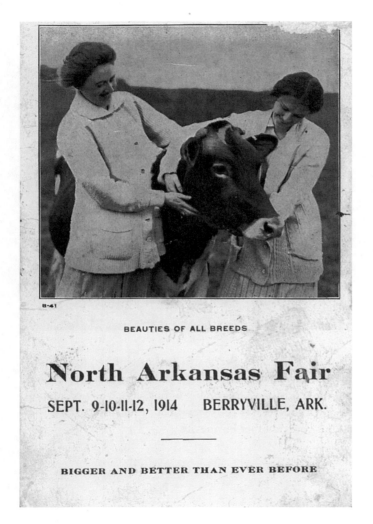

Postcards were sometimes produced to promote an event of short duration, as in the case of the 1914 North Arkansas Fair held at Berryville. The recipient of this card mailed to Iowa would almost certainly have commented about the caption, "Beauties of All Breeds."

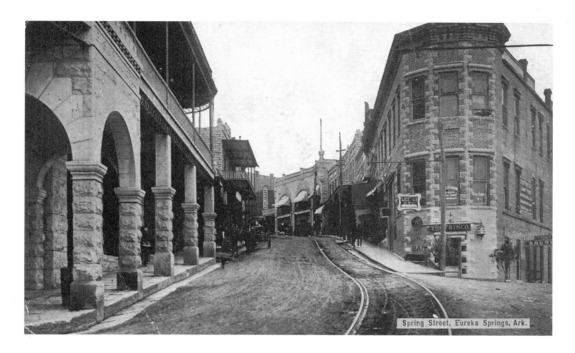

The springs and their perceived healing properties, in the area that would become known as Eureka Springs, were first widely noted during the Civil War. By the time this card was printed around 1905, the hotels, bathhouses, and winding, twisting streets had begun to draw visitors from across the nation. The Basin Park Hotel to the left still stands, while the Flat Iron building to the right, which housed the Frisco Rail offices and two saloons, was removed many years ago.

The food products used by locals and hotel guests in Eureka Springs were often supplied by surrounding farms. This postcard from around 1900 has a picture of a local merchant, apparently inspecting a farmer's eggs

One of the earlier settlers to arrive in Eureka Springs was photographer Lucian Gray, whose work often ended up on commercially produced postcards. Gray's son, who had bagged several opossums, is the subject of this 1915 postcard.

Little Photographer Gray, Youngest Opossum Hunter in Eureka Springs, Ark.

Carrie A. Nation Enjoying a Drink of Eureka Springs Water, Eureka Springs, Ark.

Eureka Springs was home to famed temperance leader Carrie Nation in her later years. In this card the woman who had a reputation for breaking up saloons with a hatchet was seen pouring herself a glass of water at a spring across the street from her home.

After its 1883 completion, the Missouri and North Arkansas Railroad brought thousands of visitors to Eureka Springs. This turn-of-the-century view shows visitors posed with a train in the "narrows," a cut through a limestone bluff adjacent to the White River, near the town of Beaver.

The economy of the remote Madison County village of St. Paul was supported by hardwood timber from the surrounding mountains. On this 1912 card young boys posed at the schoolhouse gate, with a white frame church to the left. The town reportedly had no high school; the few students from this school who went on to high school would have probably attended the one at Huntsville, the county seat.

One of the men leaning on this Missouri and North Arkansas Railroad locomotive apparently wrote the card, penning, "Have decided Harrison needs me now more than Fort W." The ill-fated railroad reached Harrison in 1901; it was never profitable and was considered the most controversial railroad in Arkansas history, with frequent wrecks and washed-out tracks. Boone county residents were known to say M&NA actually stood for "may never arrive".

The photographer caught a familiar scene around 1905, with a group of well-dressed worshipers leaving church after a Sunday sermon. In this case the congregation is from the Christian Church of Harrison.

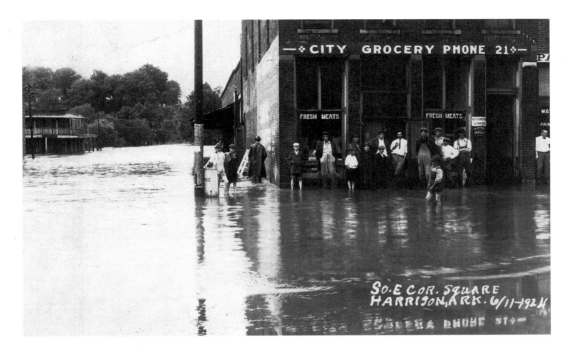

Crooked Creek near Harrison has long been a prize stream for smallmouth bass, but at times it caused the town misery. In June of 1924 the creek surged out of its banks, flooding part of the business district. In this view are seen two victims of the rising waters, the City Grocery and a hotel on the far left.

The Harrison fire chief and his wife proudly drove the town's new firetruck, flags flying, through town around 1915. Firetruck number one very likely replaced older horse-drawn equipment and would have been a source of pride in the Boone County seat.

During the early years of the century, much of the nation's produce, as well as its whisky, was transported and stored in barrels. Many of the hardwood staves that formed these barrels came from the forests of the Ozarks. In this photo from 1900, wagons are fording the Buffalo River near Jasper with a load of wood that would be milled into staves. It took generations for the forests of what is now a national park to recover from this intense harvest of timber.

The Buffalo River that flowed through Newton County would one day be a nationally known scenic float stream. In the early 1900s it was a source of food, as shown by this lucky fisherman carrying a twenty-four-pound catfish down a road in Jasper.

NORTH-CENTRAL ARKANSAS

Baxter, Cleburne, Fulton, Independence, Izard, Marion, Searcy, Sharp, Stone, Van Buren, and White Counties

North-central Arkansas, in the center of the Ozark Mountains, entered the century as a remote, isolated region with no paved roads and without the larger communities found in the counties to the west, such as Fayetteville. Numerous postcard subjects were found in the resort town of Heber Springs, the region's only real tourist draw, with its small Victorian hotels and the Little Red River, which would remain free-flowing until the 1960s.

Baxter and Marion counties, today noted for huge impoundments on the White River, contained only remote hamlets. The towns of Searcy and Batesville were beginning to develop industry, and both were home to private colleges. All in all, this was a region with great potential—but one that would be slower to realize its potential than other parts of the state.

"This is one of the means of transportation near Mountain Home," observes the 1909 message sent from the Baxter County seat. The White River would not be bridged in the area until around 1930, and the river was untamed until the great dams of the 1940s were constructed. Ferries were therefore an essential part of life in remote Baxter County.

The Baxter County Fair, Buford, Ark. SEPTEMBER 25, 26, 27, 1912

The Baxter County hamlet of Buford had its start in 1870 when a wagon train of Mississippi settlers bound for Texas changed their minds upon receiving word of a drought in the Lone Star State. George Osborn named the town for one of his sons when the first post office was located on his farm. The town of Buford organized and put on the first Baxter County fair in 1911; this card was made for the fair of 1912.

"This is one of the street scenes. It looks quite different to the ones in Portland tho," says a 1909 message to Oregon. The narrow dirt lane passing the Baxter County Courthouse to the left and leading farther into Mountain Home, was typical of turn-of-the-century wagon roads in the area. The courthouse was torn down in the 1940s.

The town of Cotter was incorporated in 1904 with a surprisingly large population of six hundred, though many lived in tents. The night after two panthers prowled through town, there was a rush to build more substantial housing. This cabin was captured on a 1906 card sent to Texas. Today Cotter is often called the rainbow trout capital of the world; the river is tamed and made cold by huge dams.

The back of this ca. 1910 card billed Heber Springs as "The All-Year Health and Pleasure Resort. No mosquitoes, no malaria, Air laden with pine and cedar. Iron, Sulphur, and Pure Spring Waters." The building shown housed Dr. Cyrus Crosby's office upstairs with his drugstore on the lower left displaying valentines in the window. The resort town's post office is on the lower right.

Hotel Adrian. Heber Springs, Ark.

The arrival of the railroad in Heber Springs in 1908 brought a large increase in tourist traffic, and several hotels went up to accommodate the visitors. Dr. Crosby erected the Hotel Adrian, naming it for his daughter and giving it such features as a private dining room for parties, a lovely lobby, and two parlors.

The Hotel Adrian met a fiery end in 1916, a fate common to most of the early hotels that served the Cleburne County seat. The photographer captured this shot of the inferno engulfing the hotel, taken through a ladder being carried from one of the town's horse-drawn fire-fighting wagons.

From Heber Springs in 1915 came of this portrait of a newlywed couple, with the comment, "You will no doubt recognize the faces on the other side of this card. This is not good however but most of the fault is in the developer which I used.... Well they are on a farm near Hiram and seem to be quite happy and contented." The photographer had turned his own work into a postcard.

"I am still tore up, my house is not finished yet," came the cryptic note on this card from the Fulton County seat of Salem in 1910. The town, founded in 1900, would have counted among its largest business buildings W. M. Castleberry's three-story mercantile on the left. Other businesses in the photo are a drugstore, and Adley Come's Cash Merchant store on the far right.

The city of Mammoth Spring took its name from the spring that gushes 200 million gallons of water per day and forms the Spring River. At the turn of the century this water powered the Mammoth Spring Milling Company, seen on the right, that boasted a capability of producing five hundred barrels of flour per day. The mill is gone today, while the site of the spring is a state park.

"Just been out for a walk we are going to the show tonight," reads the 1913 message sent on the back of a view of the crowded main street of Mammoth Spring. Visible on the card is a car with license plate number 834. Both wagons and automobiles share the rutted dirt street. One of the boys in the center carries a stick bearing a can, perhaps of sorghum.

Originally Napoleon, then Poke Creek, the name of the county seat of Independence County was changed to Batesville in 1824, twelve years before Arkansas statehood. The city prospered at the turn of the century, and its main street is today recognized for the preservation of many of the historic buildings seen in this card from around 1915. The man standing beside his buggy looking at the automobile-lined street may have reflected on the rapidly changing face of his town.

The small town of Batesville had for many years two orphanages; this one, operated by the Independent Order of Odd Fellows, was known as the Home for Widows and Orphans. The other facility in the city was operated by the Masonic Lodge; it operated until 1947, while the Odd Fellows' facility closed around 1930.

The staff of the Odd Fellows' Home for Widows and Orphans took pride in giving its residents the opportunity to showcase their talent. Such was the case with the "Orphan Boys Band" that traveled in 1915 on what must have been the Batesville facility's version of a bus.

On April 21, 1920, fire broke out in the Vine Street home of Batesville resident H. Carpenter. A high wind soon pushed the flames beyond the capacity of the town's volunteer fire department to control it. The handsome homes of thirty of the wealthiest families in town were destroyed, along with some fifty other buildings—leaving an estimated three hundred people homeless.

The Confederate monument was unveiled on the courthouse lawn in Batesville in 1907 to honor the Arkansas men in gray who had fought in the Civil War, which had ended only forty-two years before. Almost certainly some of that war's veterans are in this photo. The ceremonious placement of Confederate monuments made for a festive occasion in a number of Arkansas communities during the early years of this century.

The preferred form of transportation in the Ozark foothills was the frequent passenger trains that served the region. Around 1910 a well-dressed woman was photographed at a wagon road crossing the tracks near Batesville. She is apparently flagging down the train with her raised umbrella in an early-day equivalent of hailing a taxi or catching a bus.

Among the major employers in Independence County was Pfeiffer's Stone Quarry near Batesville. Heavy slabs of marble were sawed from the quarry and apparently moved for shipment across the rail bridge shown here. Stone from the area went into the state capitol in Little Rock, which was nearing completion around the time the card was printed, in 1910.

"Dear Friend, Well here we are and it is fine," came the 1908 words from the Park Hotel in Yellville, seat of Marion County, named for Gen. Francis Marion, a hero of the American Revolution. To the right of the two-story hotel is the sample room, where traveling salesmen lodging at the hotel could display their wares.

High School at Yellville, Ark.

"Your card came glad to get it. I have been sick a week. They have 3 cases of small pox here. . . . This is the picture of the school that I attend," reads the 1916 message sent from Yellville to Little Rock. That year Yellville would have been one of the five thousand school districts recognized in the state of Arkansas at that time, an astounding number in today's era of school-district consolidation.

The Searcy County town of Leslie was home to the H. D. Williams Cooperage Company mill, which was the largest barrel factory in the world. Hundreds of men worked in the plants and in the woods. The rail line, shown here in 1910, was built by Williams to haul timber from the headwaters of the Little Red River. The intriguing message reads in part, "I can sit in my window and see the Legislature is in session and now we are to have electric lights." The card was mailed from a train, most likely by a passenger just passing through Leslie.

The nation's rapidly expanding railroads created a great demand for wooden ties to support the growing network of tracks. The plentiful white oak forests of the Arkansas Ozarks met much of this demand, as evidenced by these hard-working men loading the heavy ties into railcars at Leslie around 1910.

The town square of the Searcy County seat of Marshall was the subject of this postcard in 1925. The courthouse is just out of view to the left, while the building to the center right, with Coca Cola signs and gas pumps, was the Buck Mays General Store. Later a department store, the establishment served the town for decades, closing only in 1994.

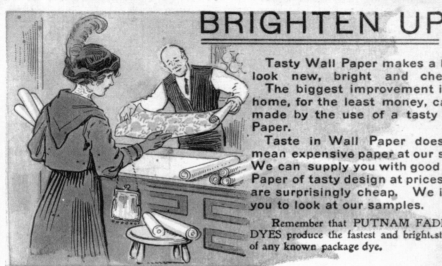

Wallpaper was a popular, much-marketed product for Arkansas homes constructed in the early years of the century. The R. H. Wayland and Son store in the small Izard County community of Pineville mailed out these cards around 1905 promoting good taste in wall paper with "fadeless" dyes.

The Spring River flowed out of Fulton County into Sharp County, where the reflection of a Frisco locomotive pulling a long string of boxcars was captured around 1910, in the waters of what would become one of the state's most popular recreation streams decades later.

The White River bluff-top town of Calico Rock was named for the multicolored limestone bluffs that lined the river in the area. "West of town, looking toward the depot," is the 1909 message, probably written by one of the well-dressed women standing near the edge of one of the "calico bluffs"; the women were surely mindful of their children's safety, being situated so near the edge.

The small Sharp County town of Evening Shade would come to the nation's attention in the 1990s as the setting for a TV sitcom starring Burt Reynolds. Around the turn of the century most townspeople got their drinking water from the town spring which, according to the card, generated 21,600 gallons of water per day. An area doctor arranged to have the spring walled in and protected as shown here, but eventually it would dry up and be covered over.

The Stone County seat of Mountain View had muddy, rutted streets on the day around 1900 when a photographer captured this image that included the Bank of Mountain View to the left, J. B. Hannah's store in the center, and Dr. Lee Welch's Drugstore to the right. Ownership of the local drugstore by the town's doctor was not uncommon in this era.

An unidentified employee of the Van Buren County Bank in Clinton posed for this photo in 1910—the year indicated by the wall calendar. Note the telephone and the man's adding machine, which he used as he sat at his roll-top desk. In later years the bank would move out, and the building, complete with vault seen in the background, would become a law office.

Searcy, seat of White County, was laid out in 1837, a year after statehood, and named for Richard H. Searcy, a prominent lawyer and judge. This card showing both the public school and courthouse was mailed to Ontario, Canada in 1911. The White County Courthouse, built in 1870, is today the oldest functioning courthouse in the state.

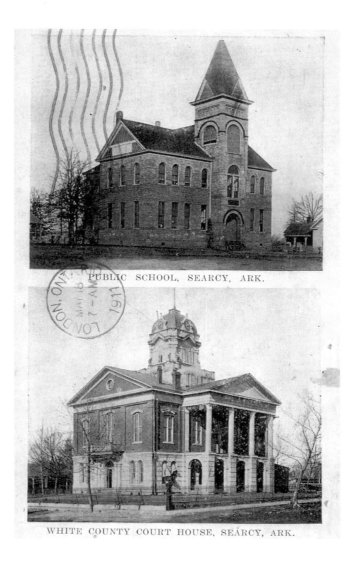

PUBLIC SCHOOL, SEARCY, ARK.

WHITE COUNTY COURT HOUSE, SEARCY, ARK.

During the first two decades of the century, according to the Arkansas Commissioner of Mines, Manufacturers and Agriculture, seventy-three of the state's seventy-five counties grew cotton. This farmer is seen hauling one of his bales into Searcy by means of ox-drawn wagon in 1908, likely for rail shipment to a cotton gin.

"This makes two letters and two cards I have sent to you and haven't heard a word. I'm getting worried," was the 1910 message from Beebe. The White County town was named for Roswell Beebe, who originally owned the land in Little Rock upon which the first Arkansas capitol was built in the 1830s.

The City Dray was photographed at the Bald Knob depot in 1911. A drayman would have been employed to haul freight from the rail station, delivering it to area merchants and manufacturers, whose goods mostly moved by rail in this era.

The legless man who posed in 1912 in the White County town of Judsonia was said to have the last name of Rose. As he traveled across the nation, in this case en route to Ohio, he sold postcards along the way to pay his expenses. Ada Morris of Cabot recalled in 1994 that Rose stopped by her mother's house for a charitable meal when she a girl of eight years old.

In 1907 a group of senior citizens posed for a group photo at what was billed as an "Old Folks Reception" at Judsonia. Some of these people would have been alive before Arkansas achieved statehood in 1836, and all would have had vivid memories of the American Civil War.

Two men building a house paused for the photographer in Judsonia around 1910. The work was hard, the days were long, and power tools were still in the future—but the house would have been built for only a few hundred dollars, in all likelihood.

Travel by road in rural Arkansas in 1910 usually was as shown in this card mailed from Cave City with the message, "Hello Cousins, this was the trip I made to St. Joe [Searcy County] while you were here." Among the items on Sam Stephen's wagon are a large barrel and a skillet.

NORTHEAST ARKANSAS

Clay, Craighead, Crittenden, Cross, Greene, Jackson, Lawrence, Mississippi, Poinsett, and Randolph Counties

At the turn of the century, northeast Arkansas was still largely covered with great bottomland hardwood forests. The forest was rapidly being cleared, and where massive oaks once grew, farms and towns began to take shape. Postcard subjects included massive logs being hauled to mills, rice fields, cotton plantations near Blytheville, and many new business districts.

Frequently photographed for postcards was the commerce on the White River at Newport, especially the bustling mussel business that produced both pearls and barge loads of shells that were turned into buttons. River traffic was photographed on streams that today are not navigable, such as the Black River at Corning, where steamboats once docked. Schools, churches, new courthouses all found their way onto postcards, along with the all-important trains such as those that created the need for the rail hub in the Lawrence County town of Hoxie.

Northeast Arkansas was an untapped region of great natural resources at the turn of the century. It was poised to grow, diversify, and change radically as the heavy hand of man and his technology converted a great virgin forest into jobs and raw materials for the entire nation. Much of this activity was recorded on postcards that allow present-day Arkansans to see the profound changes their state underwent in the early years of the century.

"We are seldom ever sick, so you see it is healthy out here," was the 1910 message sent from the Clay County town of Piggott to Commodore Fallowfield of Weed, California. The town, one of two Clay County seats, is seen on this montage showing the courthouse, the business district, and a local deer-camp scene.

Piggott, ca. 1905. Sometimes postcards captured images of small-town Arkansas churches with very unusual architecture. Such was the case with the Christian Church of Piggott. The building was constructed of brick, was adorned by a six-sided bell tower, and had two unusually shaped chimneys for the fireplaces that warmed the worshippers.

W. S. QUAY BOAT ON HISTORIC BLACK RIVER NEAR CORNING, ARK.

Corning, ca. 1911. The Black River was navigable in the early part of the century, but accidents did happen, such as this one when a wooden-hulled boat hit an underwater snag. Here efforts are underway to raise the unfortunate vessel. The river has not been navigable for larger boats for many years but does provide recreation for the area today.

Corning, ca. 1912. This card shows the business district of the second county seat of Clay County, an honor that is shared with Piggot. The only activity seems to be a horse-drawn wagon backed up to a store for loading and a lone woman talking to two men; a hotel is on the right. The town's population was around fourteen hundred, many of whom worked in a flour mill, a stave factory, a pearl-button factory that used river-mussel shells, or four sawmills that helped convert the surrounding hardwood forests to cropland.

Rector, ca. 1910. Perhaps the most unusual city park attraction in Arkansas was Motsingers Park. On what was probably a Sunday afternoon, many well-dressed children were gathered around the monkey cage, complete with a small house. The attraction reportedly has been gone for many years.

Between 1862 and 1885 Craighead County lost three courthouses to fires, one of them set by an arsonist. In the third fire not only were all records destroyed but also seven barrels of molasses that had been stored there for the winter. In 1885 this distinctive brick courthouse was built on the town square; it would serve until 1933 when it was torn down to make way for the current courthouse.

Today Jonesboro, with a population of almost fifty thousand, is among the state's major cities. In 1910, about the time this card was made, it had seven thousand residents. Students attended this two-story frame high school.

Jonesboro, ca. 1911. In an era long before the rise of great chain stores, local retailers tended toward the small and personal, such as the Eagle Clothing House for Men. The window to the right displays hats, the one to the left suits.

14479 Interior View of Eagle Clothing House, Taylor Puryear, Jonesboro, Ark.

Jonesboro, ca. 1909. An interior of the Eagle Clothing House shows what would have been one of the finer men's clothiers in northeast Arkansas. The sales clerks would have been stationed around the center counter. The glass-front cases and carefully arranged tables of pants, shirts, and hats are to the left; suits are at the rear.

Jonesboro, ca. 1905. The Craighead County seat was not without centers of culture and entertainment. At the time this photo was taken, the Malone Theatre was hosting a performance of Othello and selling Owl Cigars for five cents. The wagon parked before the playhouse was from City Bill Posters, likely delivering some posters of upcoming productions.

"This is a picture of the Sisters Hospital here. They also have a Sisters school and teach both english and German," reads the 1907 message to New York. The Olivetan Benedictine Sisters had come to Jonesboro in 1900 to give the area its first adequate hospital. It quickly became a community institution and today is the major medical center for northeastern Arkansas.

Real estate speculators printed this card around 1910 with the advertisement, "LANDING AT OTWELL, ARKANSAS. Looks like they had come to stay awhile, don't it? It takes pluck and energy to turn that great forest into farms. These young men look like the proper article. When 500 such sturdy specimens become interested in any one locality, something is bound to happen isn't it? . . . Even a single lot will be a starter for you. . . . If this interests you, send for a copy of OTWELL'S FARMER BOY, that tells all about the Farmer Boy Colonies—FREE." Will Otwell of Carlinville, Illinois, produced the cards and apparently named the town after himself. The still very small town sits today on Highway 49 in southern Craighead County.

SPENCER HARRIS STORE, NETTLETON, ARK.

"Our Appeal for your patronage is in our values. Know Them."

In 1958 Nettleton would be annexed into Jonesboro, but in 1910 it was a small independent community. Many of the locals shopped at the Spencer Harris Store. Its motto was "Our appeal for your patronage is in our values. Know them." Among the dry goods, clothing, and shoes are some hats in the foreground that appear to be some kind of sombrero.

Nettleton was founded in the St. Francis River bottoms in 1893 with the coming of the railroad. Two stave mills, a handle factory, and the Wisarkana Lumber Company (seen here in 1911) would clear the great hardwood forests in less than thirty years, at which point the economy turned from timber to rice and other crops.

Cash, ca. 1909. As seen in this view of the small Craighead County village, the clearing of the vast hardwood forests of northeastern Arkansas was hard, messy work. Most likely these men, one of whom is wearing a tie, were clearing a swamp that would later be drained for farmland. To the upper left a worker, holding an ax on his shoulder, is balanced on a floating log.

Marion, ca. 1914. Crittenden County was created in 1825 and named for Robert Crittenden, first secretary of the Arkansas Territory. The county seat of Marion was selected in 1837, a year after statehood, and named for Marion Tolbert, who platted the town. This postcard of the three-story public-school building was sent to Missouri by a child to her grandfather.

Wynne, ca. 1909. The bleak message sent to North Carolina is, "Just heard about poor Wilber being dead. . . . Mr. Jno. Bene at Wittsburg was killed and was found dead in his store the next morning, They don't know who did it." The town's dirt street shows nothing but men on horseback and wagons.

Scene on Merriman Ave. Wynne

Cross County took its name from Col. David Cross, colonel of the Fifth Arkansas Infantry of the Confederate Army during the Civil War. A 1910 view of the county seat of Wynne, the towered courthouse in the distance, was taken looking up Merriman Avenue, the main thoroughfare.

"Mother isn't expected to live and I am sitting up every night," reads the 1910 message from the Greene County seat of Paragould. The card had been produced in 1908, contrasting the new First Christian Church with its more modest predecessor of 1886 shown in the inset.

"Please exchange postals with an Arkansas girl," was the request of the sender of this postcard with a photo of a large parade, sent from Paragould to New York in 1907. The town's name was a combination of the names of two railroad barons whose tracks crossed and gave rise to the city in 1883: Jay Gould and J. W. Paramore.

Marmaduke, ca. 1909. This small Greene County town was home to the Cavitt Building, which housed a furniture store, an undertaker, and a restaurant on the left, and the fraternal hall lodge on the right. In the center a lantern is mounted on a post, seemingly a makeshift street light, perhaps for the undertaker.

Newport, ca. 1900. The Jackson County seat was founded by the railroad in 1872 on the banks of the White River. Rutted Front Street was the main business artery and featured bargains for lunch when this photo was taken: "Big meals 20 cents" are advertised on the right. An establishment further up the street had hung a sign meeting the price of its competitor. Today the street is largely vacant, the business district having moved out along Highway 67.

Newport, ca. 1912. "How is little old New York? Not nearly as quiet and peaceful as this I'll bet a pretzel," is the message on a card showing barges loaded with White River mussel shells. The shells were harvested by the ton for the occasional pearl but mostly to provide raw material for the pearl-button industry that would die out with the advent of plastic buttons later in the century.

On a cold February night in 1916, the White River's levees broke, as had been expected for several days; much of the town had already been evacuated. A family, their boat riding low, was photographed near a home on Newport's Main Street. The Jackson County Courthouse is visible at the upper right.

Newport, ca. 1915. The town's railroad and its White River location facilitated the logging of most of the area's virgin hardwood forests. The train would bring the oak and walnut logs to waiting barges, and a specially equipped steamboat would lift them from rail to river conveyance. In a few years most of the forest was gone, replaced by vast farm fields.

WRECK AT DIAZ, ARK.

"Here was quite a wreck. I saw it shortly after." The town of Diaz was located near Newport, a rail center in Jackson County. The wreckage had apparently just been shoved off the tracks to enable the rail traffic to continue, as was essential in 1915 to move both passengers and freight.

The small Lawrence County town of Imboden was named for Benjamin Imboden, who settled in the area in the 1820s. This 1910 card pictured a common rural Arkansas event, a baptizing, this one in the Spring River. The many spectators were afforded a view from atop the nearby iron bridge.

"Only car in Hoxie, one man is conductor and motorman," is the 1915 message from Lawrence County. An electric railway ran between Hoxie and adjacent Walnut Ridge for a number of years, until rendered obsolete by the automobile.

Walnut Ridge, ca. 1912. The Lawrence County seat had been laid out in 1873 by the St. Louis, Iron Mountain and Southern Railroad Company. The name was derived from the many walnut trees that covered the rolling terrain. In the distance on the dirt Main Street is the electric railcar that connected Walnut Ridge and Hoxie.

Osceola, which dates from 1836 and was named for the Seminole chief, is one of the two county seats of Mississippi County; the other is Blytheville. This 1912 card pictures the courthouse under construction; the dome was yet to have its ornate trim applied. Note the men precariously perched on the ledges around the building that still serves the county today.

Osceola, ca. 1913. A popular view of small-town Arkansas for postcards was from atop the county courthouse. Such was the case with this view looking down on Morris and Company drygoods store and the rooftops of the town.

Osceola, ca. 1912. "This view is of a town five miles south of here where I spent a very pleasant afternoon. We went to a floating theatre on the river Mon. night. Eva is having lots of auto rides." The Main Street of Osceola was still dirt, but times were changing: one automobile is in view, and a garage has already opened on the right.

"Dear Mother, Murphy and I just ready to drive out to the swamps to work. That is at the depot in the town. Some place eh?" The men most likely were at work draining and clearing the great swamps that still covered much of Mississippi County when this card was mailed near the small town of Joiner in 1912.

Blytheville, ca. 1917. It was common for the homes of prominent local residents to appear on postcards. Such was the case with the large white frame home of J. G. Sudbury, president of the Bank of Blytheville.

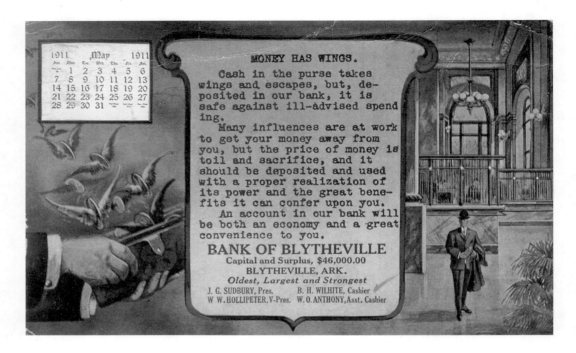

J. G. Sudbury's handsome home was paid for in part from the profits earned by soliciting deposits to add to the touted capital and surplus of forty-six thousand dollars of the "Oldest, Largest and Strongest" bank. The 1911 calendar card's advice included "Cash in the purse takes wings and escapes."

Blytheville, ca. 1914. "Logging near Blytheville, mammoth oak log, 12 feet long, scaled 2160 feet" [referring to board feet of lumber]. The labor of man and beast in extracting such trees from the dense forests can be vividly imagined when viewing this card.

Marked Tree, ca. 1910. The local postman is seen loading his buckboard in front of the Poinsett County town, said to have been named for a tree marked to indicate a safe river crossing. Among the occupants of the building is a grocery and meat market. The building no longer stands.

Marked Tree, ca. 1910. The town's location on the banks of the St. Francis River had its drawbacks, as when the flood waters rose into the grocery and meat market. The post office seen in the previous photo of the same building is absent. Likely, this photo was taken before the post office was added to the side of the building.

BUSINESS SECTION, THE TORN UP WALKS SHOW WHERE THE NEW CONCRETE PAVEMENT IS BEING LAID. MARKED TREE. ARK.

The concrete pavement alluded to on this card of Marked Tree in 1910 most likely referred to the sidewalks, not the street. Among the businesses that would benefit would be the Arkansaw Drugstore to the left and the saloon in the center of the photo.

Harrisburg, ca. 1919. This card was sent to Ohio with a message written in German commenting on the sign pointing to Daws Garage. The low fence in the center of the photo is painted to promote the local "Airdome" or outdoor theater where plays and perhaps early silent films were viewed.

The courthouse square of the Poinsett County seat was captured on a card mailed in 1912. Among items of interest the day the shutter snapped were the mule-drawn wagon parked in front of a "consolidation sale" on the right and a bathhouse to the left next to a restaurant. The X marks the building where the card's sender worked.

"Greetings from your Brother Charley," reads the 1909 message. The once-extensive forests of Poinsett County ended up in lumberyards like this one in which mule-powered wagons were used to move the loads. The finished lumber products, for the most part, would have been shipped by rail to points east and north.

Pocahontas, ca. 1900. The local photographer was quickly on the spot when a train jumped the tracks and turned over in front of the depot in the Randolph County seat. The string of passenger cars behind the engine and wrecked tender car seem to have remained on the tracks, though the fear that raced through the passenger compartments is easily imagined.

Pocahontas, ca. 1900. A suspendered wagon driver is taking a load of supplies from the Pocahontas Produce Company, which, among other products, wholesaled flour and meal. A peeling poster on the side of the building promotes the local opera house. [Card courtesy of Richard Byrne of Little Rock.]

"Was glad to hear that you passed your 'exams' all right. Here's wishing you all possible success in your work at West Point," is the 1909 message sent to a young man in Lowell, Arkansas. By 1914 he might have been an army officer on the eve of the outbreak of World War I. The small Randolph County town of Biggers housed its visitors at the Ida May Hotel, some of whom surely commented on this mule pulling a plow down the street. Today no trace of the hotel remains.

"We expect to leave Ravenden Springs and turn our noses homeward Saturday, will reach Moline [Illinois] Sunday," reads the 1907 message from the remote Randolph County village of Ravenden Springs. The businesses intermingled with homes along the rough dirt road included a hardware store to the left and a clothing and shoe store in the center.

EASTERN ARKANSAS

Lee, Monroe, Phillips, Prairie, St. Francis, and Woodruff Counties

EASTERN ARKANSAS, with its antebellum homes, vast farms, and rail lines connecting Little Rock with Memphis, produced postcards from bustling towns like Marianna, Forrest City, and Brinkley. The Phillips County seat of Helena produced more turn-of-the-century postcards than any place in eastern Arkansas, with subjects ranging from the many steamboats docking before the city on the Mississippi to an opera house, parades, the Cherry Street business district, and a lumber industry that thrived as the surrounding river bottoms were cleared of massive cypress and oak trees.

In an era before passable roads were built, the railroads were vital to eastern Arkansas and were much in evidence on postcards. Views of depots and adjacent hotels and track construction were common, as were messages that were often written on the moving trains. All of these speak of the importance of the railroad in Arkansas life. Their message speaks long after the last whistle has faded and after most of the tracks have been removed, replaced by interstate highways that speed motorists by flat fields of row crops stretching into the distance, where once primeval swamps and great trees stood.

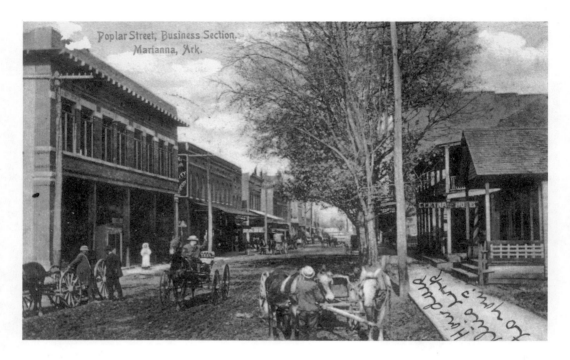

Marianna, county seat of Lee County, was incorporated in 1877 and flourished because of the junction of two rail lines and the surrounding farm economy. This 1908 card captured a view of a muddy, wagon-lined, and busy Poplar Street, heart of the town's business district. The message written on the sidewalk in front of the Central Hotel is, "How does this look to You?"

A 1911 postcard captured the image of a well-dressed couple, perhaps the owners, visiting a cotton farm outside Marianna. The message sent to Missouri states, "I have bought a 400 A. farm." By 1920 the state was producing up to a million bales of cotton a year, valued at some $180,000,000, a factor that led to extensive clearing of bottom-land forests in Lee and other eastern Arkansas counties, as more landowners sought to profit.

Hazen, ca. 1916. The Kocourek and Son Hardware and Furniture store was the major business in Hazen, selling buggies, furniture, hardware, and a full line of farm implements. The store is still doing business today in the same building, selling hardware and farm equipment—but no buggies.

Hazen, ca. 1910. The small Prairie County farming community's local bank and post office shared this sturdy corner building, before which is parked what would have been one of the few automobiles in town. Today the building stands vacant but otherwise unchanged on the outside.

Brinkley, seat of Monroe County, was founded in 1872 and quickly prospered, with rail lines, several sawmills, large surrounding farms, and a thriving business district. The town of some two thousand people in 1910 was home to a half-dozen churches, among which was this handsome white frame Baptist church.

At 7:07 P.M. on March 8, 1909, a tornado, then called a cyclone by many, roared through Brinkley, destroying most of the town, including almost every church. The Baptist church was left a pile of splintered lumber in the wake of a storm one newspaper labeled an "air quake" because the devastation was reminiscent of the San Francisco earthquake of 1906, three years before.

Gov. George Donaghey answered Brinkley's call for help by ordering a train load of convicts from the prison near Little Rock to be brought in to help with the cleanup. On this card armed guards are keeping watch over the prisoners working within the ruins of the Methodist church. On Sunday the townspeople held a worship service for the convicts.

The Brinkley tornado of 1909 killed thirty-five people and destroyed or damaged virtually every home or business in town, including the train station. In this card men are standing before the ruins of a store; the freakish nature of the storm is apparent in that many goods are still sitting on the shelves of the one surviving wall of the business.

Helena's major thoroughfare, Cherry Street, was the heart of the Mississippi River port city. This card, made around 1905, shows residents sharing a dirt street with chickens. To the left a store is advertising "Sensational Prices." The message on the back of the card reads, "They are decorating for Mardi Gras. They are putting 17 strings of electric lights across this street. . . . There are to be 20 floats which were used at New Orleans last year."

Many Residences of this Class in Helena, Ark.

A part of the pride of Helena was, and remains today, the fine Victorian homes erected by the people who prospered in the city. A number of postcards were produced in the early years of the century, and the images of these homes were mailed across the nation.

Helena and Phillips County have had a sizable black population since before the Civil War. It was common early in the century to show black institutions on postcards, as in this card from around 1910 featuring "Some of the Churches and Schools for Colored People in Helena, Ark."

The Mississippi River brought many impressive craft to Helena, and one frequent visitor to the dock was the *Kate Adams* which ran a regular route from Memphis to Arkansas City, stopping off in Helena to load freight and deliver mail. The ship was destroyed by fire in 1927.

Capt. Oldrieve Walking on the Water from Cincinnati to New Orleans, 1,800 Miles, on a Wager of $5,000—Passing Helena, Ark., January 25, '07.

College professor Charles Oldrieve, on a five-thousand-dollar bet, set out in the winter of 1906 to walk down the Ohio and Mississippi Rivers wearing four-foot-long "pontoon shoes" made of cedar, with his wife accompanying him in a rowboat. This card was made when he passed Helena in 1907; he arrived in New Orleans forty days after starting out, but was broken in health and died at age thirty-one.

There was no bridge at Helena in the early years of the century, but the first railroad ferries had opened in 1889. In this 1909 card, the Y. and M. V. Railway Incline demonstrated how the ferry boat carried the train across the wide Mississippi and allowed the train to drive off onto an inclined set of tracks connected to the railroad.

The St. Louis and Iron Mountain rail depot was built just inside the Mississippi River levee and served thousands of passengers over the years. When rail service ended, the depot fell into disrepair but was rescued and restored to become a museum that today houses the Delta Cultural Center, a major tourist draw in modern Helena.

Helena took its public-safety obligations seriously, erecting this combination police department and fire station. The firefighters of 1910, when this card was made, would have driven horse-drawn equipment with limited capacity to fight serious blazes.

Helena's Jefferson School was erected around 1885. This postcard shows children posed on the school grounds; the boy on the left appears to have had problems controlling a large dog. The Arkansas State Board of Education was created in 1911, the year this card was mailed.

The ad on the back of this 1910 card reads, "Good Place for You to Locate Helena, Ark—Situated in the Timber Belt of the Southwest. More timber accessible to this point than to any other one point in the United State...." The message goes on to list numerous types of trees available "in almost inexhaustible quantities," and lists Dan T. Cutting, "Industrial Commissioner," as the contact person. Today we know trees like this oak were indeed exhaustible; virtually all are gone the way of the one pictured.

Eastern Arkansas was once home to thousands of acres of virgin cypress forest; very few of the huge trees remain today in an area largely converted to farmland. The trees were milled and shipped by rail across the nation.

"May Festival is over tonight. Maybe I will have a chance to breathe. We had some good time," is the 1909 message. These Helena motorists, in a rather prophetic pose, sit in front of a horse stable which would soon be rendered obsolete.

Helena's affluence brought a level of culture and entertainment surpassing that of many larger towns. The Helena Opera House was built in 1887 and was considered one of the three finest in the South. Helena was the smallest town in the United States to be a member of the Civic Music Association. The opera house burned in the 1920s.

Habib Etoch's Delicatessen on Cherry Street was for many years the dining establishment of choice for Helena businessmen. The card, mailed in 1921, notes, "Hugh Finnegan passed away three weeks ago very suddenly. I was with him his last day. Sent for me."

Marvell Corruth, a native of Mississippi, immigrated to eastern Phillips County before the Civil War and developed a large plantation there. The city took his first name and became prosperous with the coming of the railroad in the 1870s. In this photo taken around 1915, Marvell's dirt Main Street was lined with businesses, including at least two drugstores. Today the buildings stand largely vacant.

Forrest City was incorporated in 1871 and named for Confederate General Nathan Bedford Forrest. This view of the Front Street Business District was taken from the St. Francis County Courthouse. Today most of the buildings are vacant because the business section has relocated near Interstate 40.

Forrest City's Hotel Marion had much of its bottom floor devoted to the town's train depot. Of note are the large trunks, perhaps standing ready to go out on the next train. The writer of this 1907 card chastised a Tennessee friend for not coming for a visit.

The St. Francis River provided both sport for anglers and a postcard subject as shown in this view of a successful trio with their stringers full of catfish. The clothing suggests that it was perhaps a winter day, but food on the table was the reward for any discomfort.

The Woodruff County town of McCrory, like many small towns, took pride in its local high school; such buildings often ended up on postcards. This building was apparently heated by fireplaces: a large chimney is located at each corner of the building.

Augusta, the seat of Woodruff County, had its main street captured on a 1910 card mailed to Oklahoma with the words, "I am so mad to think I had to get sick at the wrong time." The dirt street, here rutted with wagon tracks, would have been a quagmire after heavy rains and choked with dust in dry periods.

SOUTHEAST ARKANSAS

Arkansas, Ashley, Bradley, Chicot, Cleveland, Desha, Drew, Jefferson, and Lincoln Counties

SOUTHEASTERN ARKANSAS, while home to some Civil War–era plantations, was still home to vast bottomland forests in the early years of the twentieth century. These forests, and the rich farmland that developed as they were cleared, were depicted on many postcards. In Ashley County the town of Crossett was born as a timber "company town," and Bradley County carried the title of "soft pine capital of the world." The railroads that carried the logs and finished lumber also became postcard subjects.

Some of the most photographed card subjects in this part of the state were the rice-farming operations around Stuttgart. The fields, the harvests, the water wells that gave the fields life, and the mills that processed the grain that had been planted as an experiment by German immigrants in 1904 would all appear on thousands of postcards.

Pine Bluff was the most frequently captured city on southeastern Arkansas postcards with depictions of its business-lined Main Street, fine churches, a Jewish synagogue, a hospital, and many handsome public buildings. The city grew rapidly as a rail center and as a shipping point for the huge riverboats that docked on the Arkansas River that lapped at the edge of the city.

River transportation, railroads, and some of the richest soil in the world would bring about phenomenal change in what just a few years before had been largely a wilderness of swamps and great forests, and much of the transition was reflected on postcards sent across the nation.

Star City became the seat of Lincoln County in 1871, so named reportedly because all the roads converged at its site in the center of the county in the shape of a star. This photo of the town's wooden-framed high school was made around 1910, when the state's annual spending per pupil averaged twelve dollars. The building to the right is apparently an older, seemingly abandoned school.

The first successful rice crop was produced in the Grand Prairie region of Arkansas in 1904, and the economy of the region was forever changed. Early production relied on horse-drawn harvesting equipment like this caught on a postcard from around 1908.

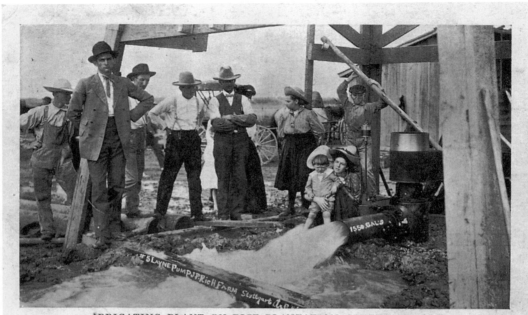

IRRIGATING PLANT ON RICE PLANTATION, STUTTGART, ARK.

Growing rice on the largely treeless Grand Prairie took great quantities of water, often supplied by wells like this one photographed in 1908. The message sent to Indiana reads, "I am going to a rice plantation near here and then am going to take a ride in the country."

The rice was harvested and brought to mills for processing and shipment by rail across the nation. The first Arkansas rice mill was established in Stuttgart in 1907 by the Reverend Adam Buerkle. The initiative would help make the city the rice capital of the world as merchants, lawyers, and others soon came to the area to support the rice farmers.

Farm families worked hard all week, but most put on their good clothes for church on Sunday. This couple posed with some rabbits on an Easter Sunday around 1910.

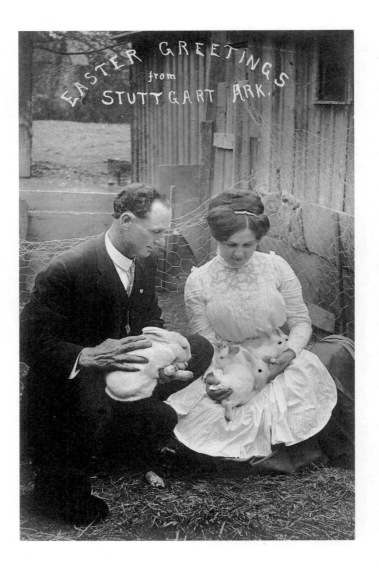

Stuttgart, Arkansas had its start in 1884 when founded by Louis Buerckle, who named it for the city in Germany where area immigrants had come from. On what was likely a busy Saturday around 1910, a crowd gathered before Helm Furniture for a demonstration of the latest Singer sewing machine. The sign indicates the Helms family also worked as embalmers and undertakers.

Stuttgart's rice-based economy fostered a prosperity that is quite evident in this 1917 view of a busy Main Street and numerous automobiles. The business on the left is a grocery store and "William's Bargain Store."

In 1916 the Mexican rebel leader Pancho Villa inspired Uncle Sam's wrath when he raided tiny Columbus, New Mexico. Soon troops were on their way to the border, creating a stir when a troop train rolled through Stuttgart.

In 1917 the nation watched the war raging in Europe with many Americans expecting the United States to be called upon to defeat the Kaiser and save France. Stuttgart was among the cities that held "Preparedness Parades" like the one shown here.

Turn-of-the-century Arkansas children, like today's, enjoyed dressing up in costumes. These youngsters posed on a Stuttgart porch include an Indian, a devil, and one that appears to be George Washington.

"This is where I teach, the room marked is mine" wrote a teacher about the Stuttgart school on a 1907 view sent to Kansas. In 1910 the average annual salary for Arkansas's school teachers was $273.

A group of children posed with their teacher outside the Stuttgart public school. Several of the children are barefoot and some appear to be wearing homespun clothing. By Arkansas law the school year consisted of 107 days in 1910, when the card was mailed.

Dewitt was named in 1854 when three Arkansas County commissioners put their names in a hat, and DeWitt Clinton's was drawn. The crowd in front of the dry goods store was likely gathered for a product demonstration. The store in the center of the photo bears a sign reading "Furniture, Coffins and Caskets," a reminder that the dead were often prepared for burial at home in this era.

Almyra was typical of the smaller farming communities in eastern Arkansas, farm houses, outbuildings, and garden plots merging to become a town along a new dirt road. The message reads, "Thought I would send you more cards . . . so you would not get so lonesome."

The Almyra public school and the local Methodist church were adjacent to each other beside a farm field stretching into the distance. The plank walk would have kept people's feet out of the mud as they came either to worship or to learn at one of the bell-topped, white frame buildings.

The thriving farm economy of eastern Arkansas helped insure that even the smallest of communities had rail service and a depot, as was the case in the Arkansas County town of Ulm. The sign above the two men advises that it is 451 miles to Waco, 408 miles to Fort Worth, and 226 miles to Cairo, Illinois.

In the early years of the century the streams and oxbow lakes of eastern Arkansas teemed with fish. These men and women used an early boat and trailer combination. This card from around 1910 says "Going home with a boat full of fish from Big Long Lake."

An obviously pleased group of lady anglers posed with their catch and their cane poles in front of the car that brought them to a lake near the Arkansas County town of Almyra around 1915.

Hamburg, the seat of Ashley County, reportedly got its name in 1849 when a deer killed nearby was said to have an especially fine set of "hams." The town grew as a lumber community capitalizing on the huge virgin forests of the area, as evidenced by the oxen-drawn logs posed in front of the courthouse in 1902.

Crossett, a true "company town," was founded in 1902 by the Crossett Lumber Company. The message on the card reads, "Send these cards so the children can see what we do in Ark." The railroad made possible the exploitation of vast amounts of timber from what had once been inaccessible wilderness.

The small village of Montrose, in Ashley County, had a compact business district with the Cone Hotel to the left and the Shipman Drug Store on the right as seen on this 1908 card. Doctor Shipman's office was on the second floor above the store, so that filling his prescriptions was quite convenient.

Warren was reportedly named for the black body servant of a local man when the town was being laid out in 1842. Timber was the mainstay of the economy, but farming played its part as seen in a 1907 view of the streets filled with cotton awaiting shipment.

By 1920 twelve lumber companies operated in the vicinity of Warren, drawn to the vast virgin forests of yellow pine. The steam-powered machine shown here was mounted on a railcar and loaded the logs aboard the flatcars for shipment to the mills.

Warren was billed as the "Largest Yellow Pine Market in the World," apparently with good reason. It was claimed that a carload of lumber was shipped every fifteen minutes the year around to markets across the nation.

Bradley County's diverse virgin forest was home to a variety of impressive trees, including this massive oak awaiting processing. The card, mailed around 1908 by a child to his teacher, says 1,692 feet of lumber came from the 12-foot log.

Today Bradley County is often referred to as the "Pink Tomato Capital of the World." The area residents discovered how well the rich soil would grow the vegetables: 400 crates per acre at prices ranging from $.65 to $1.10 per crate according to this 1910 view printed by the Cotton Belt Railroad.

Southeast Arkansas was home to much of the state's black population, including some former slaves. In this ca. 1905 photo the black business district of the Chicot County community of Eudora included C. W. Wise's Meat Market, a bakery, and a general store.

Lake Chicot formed when the Mississippi River changed course. The town of Lake Village grew up, bringing visitors from far and wide to fish and swim in the lake overlooked by the courthouse and business district. It was reported that early in the century five thousand pounds of iced fish were shipped from the lake daily to points as far away as Chicago.

The small south Chicot County community of Portland boasted a luxury not enjoyed even by many larger towns, namely a swimming pool complete with two slides, which was fed by an artesian well. The pool's users, all white, are being observed by well-dressed black girls seated on a bench next to the center slide. Today the well has long since dried up, and the pool is gone.

Part of Front Street, Arkansas City, Ark.

Arkansas City grew and prospered on the banks of the Mississippi River, a circumstance which prompted the Desha Bank (on the right) to be built off the ground to avoid flooding. Other businesses in this 1907 view include the Gambe and DeMarke Saloon in the center. Some years later the river would shift course several miles to the east, and nearby McGehee would become the dominant town in the area.

There were perhaps only twenty inhabitants when the Missouri Pacific Railroad arrived in McGehee to establish two divisions in 1905; by 1910 the population exceeded one thousand, and by 1920 more than two thousand. In this 1910 photo the businesses located near the depot included a diamond and watch store, a drugstore, and a saloon.

MAIN STREET, McGEHEE, ARK.

McGehee, like much of southeast Arkansas, marked its progress by the arrival of telephones. Here, in 1908 a worker dangles from a telephone pole. The message reads, "Don't talk about the sunny South, I just put my winter underwear on this morning and had to put my shoes on after it snowed."

Automobiles were still a novelty in 1915, and it was an occasion worthy of a postcard when the Monticello Motor Club lined up their vehicles in the dirt street of the Drew County seat.

Pine Bluff, the largest city in Southeast Arkansas, was incorporated in 1846 and had a population of around ten thousand in 1906 when this card of Main Street was mailed. The view looks from the Jefferson County Courthouse steps down a dirt street which was the heart of the business district.

Originally opened as the Hotel Trulock, this remodeled structure became the Hotel Jefferson and was considered the finest in southeast Arkansas when this 1908 card was mailed.

The lobby of the Jefferson was quite elegant with stained glass overhead and tile on the floor. The card was sent in 1911 to Hot Springs with the message, "I have a friend, Earl Bowman, who is coming over there on his motor cycle this a.m. . . . I have told him to look you up, and if he does, show him the village, for Earl is a great fellow."

"31st of Oct.! Just think! not long until Thanksgiving," is the 1909 message on the back of a card of the ladies' parlor in the Jefferson Hotel. The hotel was torn down in the 1960s; the site is now a parking lot for the courthouse.

Fire Department, Pine Bluff, Ark. Received papers, O.K. Archer

The most modern fire-fighting equipment was the pride of larger Arkansas communities, and Pine Bluff in 1906 was no exception. The uniformed men of Fire Department Number 1 pose with horse-drawn equipment. The animal below the lead horse's neck appears to be a sheep.

The first hospital in Pine Bluff was the Florence Sanitarium, a privately operated facility built for fifteen thousand dollars in 1907 and named for the wife of the owner, Dr. Arthur Clifton. The floors were served by elevators, and the rooms were cooled by electric fans. In later years the building was converted to apartments.

"You may see by this that we have some 'sports' here anyway," reads the message from a 1908 postcard with a photo taken in front of the Jefferson County Courthouse and a bank building. The first automobile had arrived in the city in 1900.

The Arkansas River flowing at the city's edge was essential to Pine Bluff's growth and provided a port of call for ships like the *Hallett,* a 161-foot-long sternwheeler. This load of cotton, in a photo taken around 1901, would have likely been bound for northern mills.

Pine Bluff's proximity to the Arkansas River was a mixed blessing as shown by this photo of the 1908 flood. The line to the right marks where the river bank had been only days earlier; before the waters subsided, the buildings in the foreground would join those already washed down the raging river. In the distance is the Jefferson County Courthouse.

The rural Jefferson County farming community of Moscow was served by M. W. Ware's Dry Goods Store and Post Office in a building erected in 1910. The crowd on the porch had gathered to pose with Mr. Ware and his automobile.

A 1914 card captured Mr. M. W. Ware, puffing a cigar, sitting in his dry goods store in Moscow. The merchandise and layout typified the small-town general store, carrying a little bit of everything. The stools, one of which Mr. Ware is sitting on, would have been used by ladies as they were shown bolts of cloth from the shelves to the left.

SOUTHWEST ARKANSAS

Calhoun, Clark, Columbia, Dallas, Hempstead, Hot Spring, Howard, Lafayette, Little River, Miller, Montgomery, Nevada, Ouachita, Pike, Polk, Scott, Sevier, and Union Counties

THE SOUTHWESTERN QUADRANT of Arkansas was dotted with rural hamlets in the early years of the century, but centers of commerce and industry had begun to arise in the larger cities of Texarkana and El Dorado. When oil was struck at El Dorado in 1921, the first true economic boom hit South Arkansas. Glass and tile factories and large churches and department stores would be among the postcard subjects sent across the nation. The Ouachita River carried steamboats at the time, and along with the lumber business, brought progress and population to towns like Malvern, Camden, and Arkadelphia, which was home to two colleges.

Among the sources of postcard pride for remote communities were the diamond mine at Murfreesboro and the Queen Wilhelmina Hotel on a mountain above Mena in Polk County. Even the smaller towns of Prescott, Nashville, Hope, and De Queen were captured for the daily mail, borne by trains and carrying images of schools, dirt streets, drugstores, and farm scenes. The area's game and fish were also a source of pride. Deer were brought into town squares draped across the saddles of hunters, and fish were taken from teeming streams whose tranquil bends would someday be drowned by huge impoundments.

Arkadelphia, ca. 1906. Henderson College was founded here in 1890 by the Methodist Church, and this building was the heart of the campus facilities at the time. In 1929 the church redirected its resources to Hendrix College in Conway, turning Henderson over to the state. Henderson State Teachers College was born and is today known as Henderson State University.

"You probably know that the college burned to the ground at 5:30 a.m. last Tuesday. . . . It certainly was exciting. I thot they'd close the school, but it is going on. We are living out in private families." The 1914 card caught the blaze at Henderson College engulfing the clock tower in the center of the building.

"Hello Annie, I am over here at last," reads the 1906 message from the Ouachita Baptist College campus, where students were raising Old Glory in front of the school's central building. The college, one of two in Arkadelphia, was founded in 1886 by the Baptist Church, on the campus of the former Arkansas Institute for the Education of the Blind.

Arkadelphia, ca. 1914. The Arkansas Razorbacks at one time played the state's smaller colleges in football. This card proclaims their loss to Ouachita Baptist College by six points, and an ad on the back of the card promotes Ouachita's next game, with Oklahoma State Normal, to be played at Hope.

Interior Clark, Sloan & Co. Drugs. - Arkadelphia, Ark.

Arkadelphia, ca. 1909. The Clark, Sloan and Company drugstore's interior appeared on a card with an ad asserting, "DRUGS. SODA FOUNTAIN. We want to be your DRUGGIST. If you doubt us, try us and we will prove it. Prompt and Courteous Attention." The soda fountain is to the right, stationery to the left.

86.—Railroad Station of Antoine Valley and Gurdon & Ft. Smith Railroads at Graysonia, Ark.

Graysonia, ca. 1905. The Clark County sawmill town once had this depot of the Antoine Valley and Gurdon and Fort Smith Railroad along with hotels and a company store. It produced millions of board feet of timber in its heyday, but when the timber was gone the town melted away, no longer existing today.

Gum Springs, ca. 1910. The tiny Clark County community boasted a train depot that had been built for six hundred dollars. A part of that cost was likely for the extra door; like most public facilities of the time, one door was marked as the "White Entrance," the other for "Colored People."

Okolona, ca. 1911. Some rural Clark County children got their three R's at the two-story school. When this photograph was made on what apparently was a winter day, a number of the students had gathered at the end of the school.

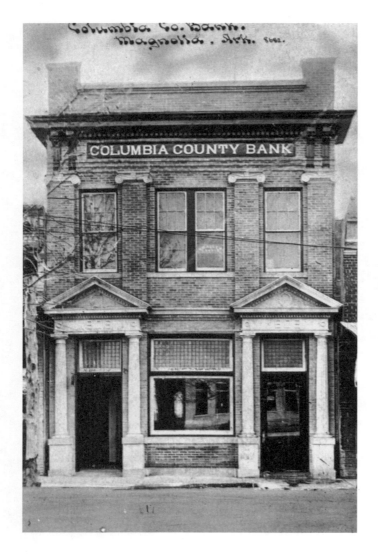

Magnolia, ca. 1905. The seat of Columbia County was chosen in 1853 and reportedly was named for a handsome grove of magnolia trees. Many of the town's citizens passed through the narrow Greek-styled doors of the Columbia County Bank.

Magnolia, ca. 1913. "Why don't some of you all write?" was an often-penned postcard message in the days before telephones became common. This card carried a view of the very unusual First Baptist Church building, now long gone.

9156 First Baptist Church, Magnolia, Ark.

Waldo, ca. 1913. "The little girl in this picture is not quite as big as you do you think," were the 1913 words from a father to his daughter. The small Columbia County town had been named by its surveyor for a railroad freight agent he had once known.

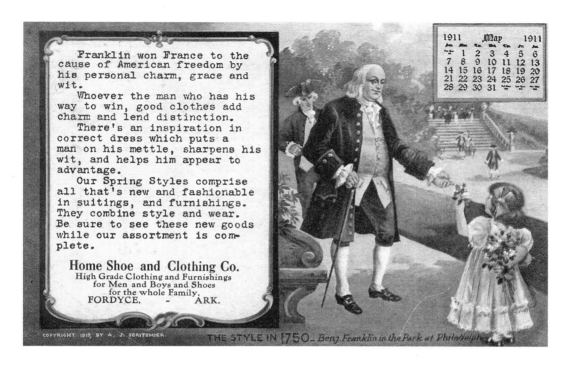

Fordyce, 1911. The Home Shoe and Clothing Company, like many small-town retailers, advertised with calendar postcards. The store used Ben Franklin to promote the virtues of a new wardrobe: "There's an inspiration in correct dress which puts a man on his mettle, sharpens his wit, and helps him appear to advantage."

Fordyce, ca. 1914. The home of prominent businessman A. Burton Banks was the subject of this postcard. Banks was the founder and president of a local insurance company, a partner in several banks, and active in the lumber business in Arkansas, Louisiana, and Canada. The home was destroyed by fire years ago.

Fordyce, ca. 1909. A. Burton Banks had not only his home on postcards but also the office building that housed his Home Accident Insurance Company. Banks's personal office was on the second floor of the building and gave him a panoramic view of Main Street. Today the handsome building still stands, largely unchanged but vacant, on Fordyce's main street.

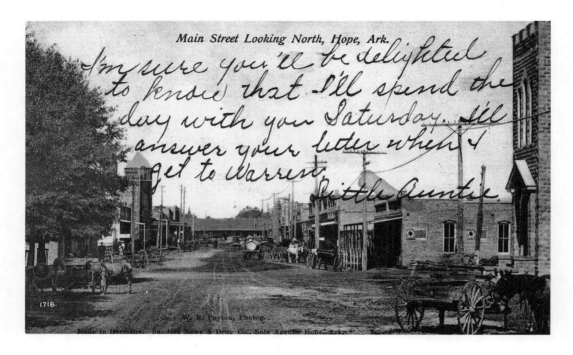

Hope, ca. 1908. The Hempstead County seat was established in 1873 and was named for the daughter of an official of the Cairo and Fulton Railroad. "Little Auntie" wrote her message on the front of this view of Main Street, with the train depot visible in the distance.

Robert La Grone's home being the subject of a postcard signified the gentleman's status in Hope around 1910. The president of the Citizens National Bank of Hope claimed to be the only person ever arrested for speeding on horseback in Hempstead County. In 1914 he was fined $5.00, plus $3.65 in court costs, for the infraction committed in Hope. Today his home no longer stands.

Bingen, ca. 1919. To France from Hempstead County went the message, "Hello Rastes how are you? . . . We are afful glad the war is over. . . . I wrote you a letter as soon as I heard you was safely across the ditch [the Atlantic]. . . . Say Rastes, I want you to be careless and don't get into any scufful with any of those French girls you may not come out as well as you did in Okla." The message could leave a present-day reader with an unsatisfied curiosity.

Malvern, ca. 1900. The Hot Spring County seat was probably named by a settler from Virginia, who was reminded of the area around Malvern Hill, Virginia, site of a Civil War battle. The wagons on the dirt Main Street are passing the city hall, the Daily News, Baker's Meat Market, and a barber shop.

"Dear Aunt," reads the 1908 message from Malvern, "I am writing you first about my appointment to the U.S. Naval Academy at Annapolis. I shall be examined in June. . . . your devoted nephew, Robt. F." In the distance, behind the Main Street business district is the Hot Spring County Courthouse; it would be torn down in the 1930s.

Malvern, ca. 1908. On the historic Rockport Bridge spanning the Ouachita River, the local militia unit posed with rifles and bayonets in hand. The bridge, built for wagons in 1900, was washed away in a flood in 1990.

Malvern, ca. 1910. A humorous photo card of six local men staging a mock brawl might have been suggested by a scene from a silent film of the era. The fourth man from the left is Alfred Bost, who operated a small grocery store in Malvern for many years.

Spruce Street, Lewisville, Ark.

Lewisville, ca. 1913. The Lafayette County seat took its name from a early settler, Lewis B. Fort, who became county judge. Today the street's buildings still stand, but many are vacant due to the ready access to nearby Hope afforded by automobiles.

Mackinaw, ca. 1910. A group of northern land speculators platted out a city near Bradley in southern Lafayette County, drawing in wide boulevards, parks, and schools. "Spec" houses like this shell were built, and prospective buyers were brought in by the train load, mostly from northern states. The venture failed, the company went bankrupt, International Paper Company bought the land, and today not a trace of Mackinaw exists.

Ashdown, ca. 1905. The Little River County seat was reportedly given its name by Lawrence Byrne, a state senator, when his sawmill and the whole community of Keller burned. Byrne remarked, "The mill is burned down and in ashes, but I am going to build a town here and call it Ashdown."

Horatio, ca. 1911. The X to the left marks the window of "Papa's" hotel room; the schoolhouse for the Little River County town is at the end of the street. Papa wrote, "Dear Little Girlie: Papa is anxiously looking for a letter from you. I do hope I will get it tomorrow. . . . I rode out about 5 mi. from town on horseback yesterday P.M. Through woods most of the way."

Texarkana, ca. 1910. The trademark Stateline Avenue pose would be used on postcards for the next forty years, to denote the street that divides Texas from Arkansas. The peg-legged man is in Arkansas with "his ass in Texas." The federal building straddling the line in the background was replaced in the 1940s.

Texarkana, ca. 1908. The Miller County Courthouse, today long gone, was embellished by the card's sender with a waving stick figure. The county was named for James Miller, a hero of the War of 1812.

Texarkana, ca. 1915. The state's larger cities worked to improve their fire-fighting capabilities, and it was a notable day when a new eight-thousand-dollar fire engine arrived with the ability to race to a blaze at "One Mile per Minute." Note the H. V. Beasley Music Store in the background, advertising the new Victor and Edison Talking Machines.

Texarkana, ca. 1908. "Sho. want to see you. . . . We are leaving for Sanitarium," reads a message suggesting that someone had tuberculosis. Broad Street was the town's principal commercial street, seen here traversed by streetcars, wagons, and many pedestrians. The store at the right prominently featured wallpaper for sale.

Miss Laura Wiley of Grapevine, Texas received this postcard in 1914 from "Cupid in Texarkana." Some publishers delighted in various word plays about the twin cities that straddle a state line.

CUPID IN TEXARKANA

When Adam and Eve first made the laws
For all the world—and Texas—
They said to Cupid "You must enforce
The line between the sexes."

"You don't know 'beans' about this game
Where hearts are trumps" said Cupid,
"And I don't care Adam for laws—
And this one is quite stupid!"

Thus in Texarkana, to observe
The line between the sexes,
The boys just stand in Arkansas
And kiss the girls in Texas.

QUINN—62

Texarkana, ca. 1911. In the era before automobiles became common, the residential streetcar lines, such as this one, were signs of a first-class city. The brief message states, "Getting a few cars here."

Texarkana, ca. 1909. "This train load of sewer pipe for Mexico shows what our neighbors on the South think of *'Tex-ark-ana'* made goods," is the message on the back of a view of the Post Pipe Company plant. "As evidence that we are not 'without honor in our country,' would greatly like an order from you—even if not for a *Train Load*!" Such manufacturing concerns were starting to put the border city on the map during this era.

Miller County, ca. 1905. A bemused look is on the face of the young fisherman, while two other boys ford the creek in a wagon. The remnants of what might have been a washed-out bridge are seen below the long cane pole.

Genoa Colony, ca. 1905. This farmer, with his wagon and team hitched and his five "stairstep" children dressed up and posed, is typical of the homesteaders of this tiny Miller County settlement. Behind the wagon is the well, and in the corner waits a freshly cut woodpile.

Genoa Colony, ca. 1905. The unpainted, wood-shingled farm house on their homestead in rural Miller County was the backdrop for this picture of members of the Powell family. The children appear to be wearing homespun clothing. The crude rock chimney is still under construction.

Slatington, ca. 1907. This photo taken in the small Montgomery County town was a typical parlor pose of the era. The floral wallpaper and rug, the wicker chair, and the photos on the wall, all suggest a family of some means for such a small town.

Mount Ida, ca. 1905. Today all these frame buildings in the Montgomery County seat are gone. The town was reportedly named by its first postmaster after a mountain in his native Massachusetts. The county is said to have been named for Richard Montgomery, an American general killed at the battle of Quebec in 1775.

Prescott, ca. 1908. The sturdy brick Bank of Prescott occupied a prominent corner in the Nevada County seat, which had been founded in 1874. The town was named by railroad officials who wanted to honor William H. Prescott, a Massachusetts author and historian.

Residence of Thomas C. McRae, Prescott, Arkansas.

Prescott, ca. 1914. Thomas C. McRae had served as the congressman from Arkansas's third district for eighteen years beginning in 1884. He would be elected governor in 1920, at the age of sixty-eight, the oldest man ever elected to the office. He served two terms and later returned to his handsome Prescott home known as "The Oaks."

"Toot! Toot! Off again. Rastus," reads the 1913 message mailed from Camden to Colorado. The train steaming into the station would take on passengers and transfer baggage and freight, including the large trunks waiting on carts beside the horse-drawn buggy that would have taken paying customers to local hotels.

Camden, ca. 1900. The site of the Ouachita County seat had been developed while still a part of the French-owned province of Louisiana because it sat at the upper end of safe navigation of the Ouachita River. What appear to be sacks of grain and barrels on the gangplank are being loaded on the steam-powered *Hank B. Hayne*. Today no commercial navigation reaches Camden.

Camden, ca. 1910. A group of mounted Confederate veterans carrying a banner was gathered for Decoration Day to honor deceased comrades. The old rebels were likely recalling events of forty-five years before, when in 1864 Camden was a Confederate fortress holding southwest Arkansas for the South.

"I am down here at Camden attending the local assembly of the Daughters of the King," reads the 1908 message on this photo of two men posed by a cannon known as "Old Betsy": "This nice old gentleman by the cannon gave us a reception at his home last night." The woman's message goes on to discuss the recent election of William Howard Taft as U.S. president. In the card's photograph, the bearded man is Joseph Reeves, and the other is John Parker, reportedly the grandson of Camden's first settler.

Camden, ca. 1912. A band marches at the head of a parade celebrating the election of Camden resident George Washington Hays as the twenty-fourth governor of Arkansas; his campaign headquarters had been in the Ouachita Hotel to the right. Hays would serve only one term.

Admiring the quality of logs. Cotton Belt Lumber Co., Bearden, Ark.

Bearden, ca. 1910. The huge virgin pine forests of Ouachita County gave rise to a timber industry that still plays a major role in the region's economy. The Cotton Belt Lumber Company's base was in the town named for John T. Bearden, an attorney for the St. Louis Southwestern Railroad.

The advertising postcard of the Cotton Belt Lumber Company, sent from Bearden in 1909, used "Parson Brown, The Spiritual Advisor" to tout the mill's products. Stereotypical casting of blacks for such purposes was not uncommon in early postcards.

Glenwood, ca. 1900. Many well-dressed children were following a wagonload of men down the dusty main street of the Pike County town. The card wasn't mailed and leaves no clue as to why everyone was gathered in the street. The many frame buildings are long gone, replaced by sturdier structures.

Murfreesboro, ca. 1910. A large crowd is out looking for gems at North America's only diamond mine, with many carrying umbrellas to deflect the sun. The first diamond had been found in 1906 by a Pike County farmer. The mine was worked commercially off and on for years, and today it is an Arkansas State Park.

"Hello Archie did you see this place before? . . . Send me some cards and I will send you some," was written in 1908 on the back of a card of the Davis block in the Polk County seat of Mena. The fashionably attired woman passing the National Bank of Mena is trying to catch up to her young son, who is pushing a baby buggy ahead of her, perhaps heading for the Grand Leader store next to the bank.

Mena, ca. 1913. The Hotel Wilhelmina was built atop Rich Mountain in 1896 by Dutch investors who named it after the queen of Holland. Although a suite was set aside for her, the queen never paid a visit. The hotel would burn twice, but was rebuilt each time; today it crowns Queen Wilhelmina State Park.

Polk County, ca. 1914. The hazards of automobile travel on Arkansas roads are well-illustrated on what must have been a cold winter day, judging by the subject's clothing. Such inconveniences led to the passage of a gasoline tax and the creation of the Arkansas Highway Commission, which worked to improve the state's roads.

Oden, ca. 1915. Before a series of dams and bridges were built, the Ouachita River was often a barrier to travelers. Near the Montgomery County town a car with "For Hire" on the windshield was shuttled across the river on a hand-pulled ferry.

Waldron, ca. 1914. It was a long-awaited day when the first telephone switchboard opened in the Scott County seat, operated by Ema Stanton. Finally those rural residents who could afford it had an alternative to letters and postcards.

"How do you think this looks for a busy day?" is the 1908 message from the Sevier County seat of De Queen. The bustling community seen here, on what almost certainly was a Saturday, had existed only eleven years when this card was mailed, having been founded in 1897 with the coming of the Kansas City Southern Railroad.

De Queen, ca. 1915. These deer hunters are posed in the dirt street in front of the office of Dr. Gore, a dentist. Rev. William Harrison, a Methodist minister seen on horseback on the far right, sent the card to his son, a student at Hendrix College in Conway.

De Queen, ca. 1907. "This is the worst looking corner in town," declared the message on this card that shows the "Burson the Buggy Man" business and Greenwald's Dry Goods and Shoes. "Well, I guess I am coming back to O.B.C.," ended the message of the college student returning to Ouachita Baptist College in Arkadelphia.

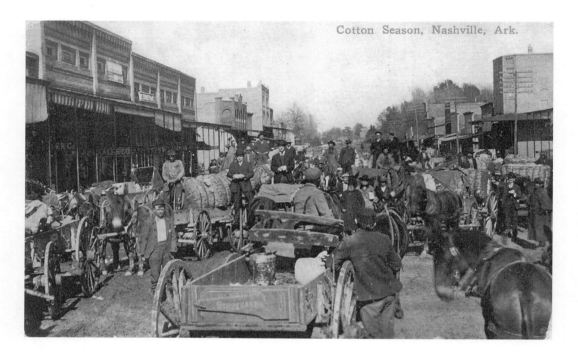

Nashville, ca. 1915. Cotton season was underway around the Howard County seat, and the crop was starting to move into town for ginning and shipping. The wagon in the foreground bears a Studebaker nameplate and carries only a can of kerosene. The town was given the name "Nashville" in 1848 by an influential settler from Tennessee, who apparently was reminded of the capitol city of his former state.

Smackover was nothing but a small flag station on the Missouri Pacific Railroad in Union County until 8:00 P.M. on May 14, 1922, when one of the largest oil strikes in the nation was made. Within a year, a thousand wells were drilled in a field that covered forty square miles, and the population had swelled from one hundred to thirty thousand. A sea of mud surrounded the hastily-erected business district, part of which is reflected in an enormous puddle on one of the many postcards produced during the boom. Today the little town's population is around two thousand, and a state museum commemorates the oil boom days.

Getting equipment into the churned-up oil fields around Smackover was an enormous task, as thousands of oil field roughnecks with tons of pipe and lumber rushed to strike it rich. Often only mules and oxen could be relied upon, as in this scene in which mules are pulling what appears to be a storage tank.

Gambling, prostitution, and other assorted forms of crime plagued the crowded oil boom town of Smackover, often overwhelming local law-enforcement officials. A committee of vigilantes, possibly members of the Ku Klux Klan, destroyed a gambling house in December of 1922 in what became known as the Ouachita War Between Saints and Sinners.

The note penciled on the front of a card showing the original Union County Courthouse refers to infantile paralysis, or polio. The disease reached epidemic levels each year in the days before the vaccine.

B. W. Reeves' Residence, El Dorado, Ark.

B.W. Reeves was the founder of a local mercantile store in El Dorado, with his seven children eventually becoming his partners. The community leader would serve as mayor of the city and be on the school board for years. His home being recorded on a postcard is a sign of his business success and stature in the community.

West Side Public Square, ElDorado, Ark.

B. W. Reeves first entered the El Dorado retail trade in 1879, erecting his store, seen at the right, on the courthouse square in 1900. His customers in this card from around 1905 seem hesitant to leave the shelter of the store awning to cross the muddy street.

El Dorado, ca. 1910. The sign on the side of this Baptist church proclaims, "A great campaign for lost souls beginning Nov. 20, 1910. U. S. Thomas, Waco, Texas will help us 'get ready.' M. W. Green, Pastor." The church was torn down many years ago but is still fondly remembered by many elderly area residents.

Baptist Church, El Dorado, Ark.

El Dorado, ca. 1922. Changes brought on by oil wealth after Arkansas' first commercially successful oil well, the "baby gusher," included paved streets. Many cars are parked before buildings that housed the El Dorado Petroleum Company, Empire Realty, the Model 5 and 10 Cent Store, and the Leader Department Store. A lone man is seen driving his wagon by the long line of parked canvas-topped black automobiles.

Arkansans have long been fascinated with crime as this photo from 1923 shows. A Union County jailbreak in 1923 was sensational enough to warrant a postcard of the cut-away bars.

Huttig, ca. 1905. The southern Union County sawmill town was named for Charles Huttig, a St. Louis banker who was a friend of the lumber company president who founded the company town. Mill workers' housing is visible in the distance, while the company store has several customers' wagons awaiting supplies on the day this photo was made.

ARKANSAS RIVER VALLEY

Conway, Crawford, Franklin, Johnson, Logan, Pope, Sebastian, and Yell Counties

THE CORRIDOR OF COUNTIES that stretches along the Arkansas River from the Oklahoma line to central Arkansas left a vivid legacy of early twentieth-century postcard history. Dominant was Fort Smith with its river traffic and the long stretch of Garrison Avenue with its banks, hotels, and occasional parades. Many residents of Fort Smith in the early 1900s had memories of federal judge Isaac Parker, the "hanging judge" who sent some seventy men to the gallows at the federal courthouse which adorned many postcards.

Van Buren, across the river from Fort Smith, produced many cards of a business district that today is restored and looks much like the turn-of-the-century postcard images, a fact that has brought new life and national recognition to the city.

The railroad had opened up the river valley in the 1880s, giving economic life to many communities. Among these were Booneville, where the state's tuberculosis sanitarium was built in 1910; Clarksville with its bumper crops of peaches; Russellville; and Morrilton, in the shadow of Petit Jean Mountain. One of the most striking postcard subjects was the Benedictine monastery at Subiaco, the founding of which had been encouraged by the railroad in order to sell adjacent land to German immigrants. The abbey, which looked much like something from Central Europe, was largely destroyed by fire in 1927 but was soon rebuilt.

Today, the river valley is bisected by Interstate 40, which connects the east and west coasts of the nation. The area is therefore traversed by much of the nation's commercial and leisure traffic. It is today a far different river valley from that of the first twenty-five years of the twentieth century, as evidenced by the postcard images that follow.

Sebastian County was created in 1851 and named for William K. Sebastian, who had been the state's first circuit judge following Arkansas's admission to the Union. Initially Greenwood was the county seat, but a tug of war among the residents eventually resulted in the main courthouse being put in Fort Smith and a smaller one in Greenwood. This courthouse from the 1880s would be replaced in the 1930s.

Fort Smith, ca. 1909. Wagons are crossing streetcar paths, with a dentist's office to the left, in this image of upper Garrison Avenue that was sent to Colorado. Mule-drawn streetcars had debuted in Fort Smith in 1883, and electric car service came in 1893 when the Fort Smith and Van Buren Electric Street Railway Light and Power Company won a franchise for service on the condition that it build a bridge across the Arkansas River connecting Fort Smith and Van Buren.

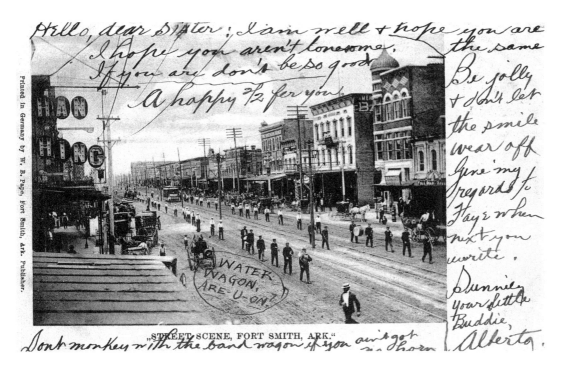

The broad stretch of Garrison Avenue was a popular, impressive parade route as shown here in 1906. The wagon is carrying two barrels, perhaps with water to settle the dust on the street. Part of the city's historic district was destroyed by a tornado in April of 1996.

Circus Parade on Gar. Ave., Ft. Smith, Ark.

Fort Smith, ca. 1906. In turn-of-the-century America, the circus train rolling into town was a cause for skipping school, and work if possible. Its acts paraded through town from the rail yard to the site of the performance, hopefully boosting ticket sales along the way. People even lined roofs in front of the Mound City Paint store to view this parade along Fort Smith's Garrison Avenue.

Fort Smith, ca. 1915. The increasing number of automobiles in Arkansas helped lead the effort to pave streets and eventually major highways. The strange-looking machine seen here was built by the Austin Manufacturing Company of Chicago and assisted in laying paving bricks in the downtown business district. Eventually most brick streets would be paved over with asphalt. A marker placed in 1913 on the courthouse lawn denoted Fort Smith as having more fifty-year-old paved streets than any other town in America. [Card courtesy of Tom Mertens of Little Rock.]

The importance of the Arkansas River to Fort Smith's economy has been central since the city's founding as a military outpost in the 1800s. In this 1910 card the packet ship *Border City* is taking on a load of potatoes for shipment, most likely moving downstream towards Little Rock. Locks and dams built on the river in the 1960s would make it much more dependable for river transport than would have been the case when the river was untamed during the earlier part of the century.

Watermelons have long been a popular summertime crop in Arkansas. The Arklavista Farm in Sebastian County delivered its melons in a wagon with a well-dressed, garter-sleeved driver, seen here around 1910. The weights of the melons had been carved onto the fruit in Roman numerals.

In keeping with its growth and emergence as a major Arkansas city, Fort Smith erected a large, ornate high school before the turn of the century. The school would suffer tornado damage, be rebuilt, and serve until a new school was erected in the 1930s; it was eventually torn down.

A group of Senior girls of the Fort Smith High School making their commencement clothes. 1914.

In the background, with hands on her hips, a teacher was photographed looking over a group of girls from Fort Smith High School sewing their commencement gowns, reinforcing skills considered essential to their future as homemakers.

"Shave and a haircut, two bits" might well have been the slogan for this Garrison Avenue barber shop around 1900. The customer seated in one of the ornate chairs seems ready for a shave from one of the young barbers.

Fort Smith, ca. 1908. "I got here all right. Edgar met me at the train. Eva well and getting along fine," was the message penned on the back of a card showing the Frisco Rail Depot. The adjacent building is painted to advertise Owl cigars for five cents. Although rail passenger service ceased decades ago in Fort Smith, the handsome depot still stands today.

St. Edward's Infirmary, with its wrap-around columned porch, was established by the Sisters of Mercy and soon became the major medical institution in western Arkansas. Today the hospital is located in a high-rise, state-of-the-art medical complex that would amaze but please the first sisters who devoted their lives to the patients who entered this handsome building.

Fort Smith, ca. 1905. Today Fort Smith is home to two major hospitals, St. Edward's Regional Medical Center and Sparks Memorial Medical Center. The latter got its start in 1887 when a charity hospital was established at Belle Point, today part of Fort Smith. Its first class of nurses graduated in 1899. A 1908 bequest of twenty-five thousand dollars in George T. Sparks's will funded a newer facility, named for Sparks. Posed on the steps in this view are the nurses who staffed the hospital at that time.

As the name suggests, Electric Park, formerly McCloud Park, was constructed in 1907 to showcase the wonders of electricity. The park with its Moorish-style architecture used fifty-six hundred electric lights and had multiple stages for entertainment. The park proved to be a boon to its sponsor, the Fort Smith Light and Traction Company, because of the many streetcar tickets patrons bought in order to reach the park, for which a twenty-five-cent admission was charged. Park attractions included a giant roller coaster, a penny arcade, boxing matches, and fireworks.

Traveling vaudeville acts of the era often performed on the stages of Electric Park. Patrons could reserve tickets at the company's office in downtown Fort Smith, travel by electric streetcar to the auditorium, and claim their tickets at the door. Streetcar service ended in Fort Smith in 1933, and the park lost much of its appeal; the buildings eventually became victims of time and neglect.

In this building "Hanging Judge" Isaac Parker presided over some thirteen thousand cases between 1875 and 1896. Of the 344 capital convictions he oversaw, 79 men were hung on the gallows near this building where most spent their final days. Today the building is a historical attraction administered by the National Park Service.

Fort Smith, ca. 1910. Between 1880 and 1890 Catholic bishop Edward Fitzgerald of Little Rock worked to help Irish Catholics immigrate from Ireland; many of these settled in Fort Smith. Their congregation erected the towering Immaculate Conception Cathedral at the head of Garrison Avenue at the turn of the century; many of their descendants still attend mass there today.

America was fighting the "war to make the world safe for democracy" in 1918, and this unidentified woman was doing her part in Sebastian county. The car has "dealer" plates, and a sign on the visor encourages all to "buy war bonds."

Mansfield, ca. 1905. Here a wagon driver poses with a load of Mason jars in the small Sebastian County town. It was very likely the jars had come in on the train and were en route to the local mercantile, where area housewives would purchase the containers for canning the fruits and vegetables from their orchards and gardens.

Mansfield, seen here around 1900, was named for W. W. Mansfield, a noted western Arkansas jurist who would serve on the state supreme court. On the day this photo was made, a frontier parade was in progress; a mounted Indian chief in a war bonnet is galloping his mount past a large sign promoting Selz Royal Blue Shoes.

Hartford, ca. 1913. "Preparing to spread shale" was the explanation of what the work crew, aided by mules, was doing in Sebastian County. The shale would have been used in an attempt to improve roads that could be almost impassable to wagons after a heavy rain.

Hackett, ca. 1900. A homesteader named Jeremial Hackett migrated from Ohio to Sebastian County in 1834 to settle at Hickory Grove. The town would take his name in 1876, and at the turn of the century this village located in the northern end of the county would boast not one, but two train depots.

"Come In," invites the sign over the Greenland, Arkansas, store of Frost and Williams. The sign "Small profits is what talks" surely aided in attracting Sebastian County shoppers to the business that sold hardware, harness, and other merchandise. Rolls of recently delivered wire lie in the dirt street.

"Greetings dear from this burg," were the words sent in 1910 to Maine from the Crawford County seat of Van Buren. Caught in a moment of time was this young boy on a bicycle among the wagons, with the train depot in the distance and the Leader Clothing store having a "Mid-Summer Sale." Today the town is nationally renowned for the restored historic downtown Main Street.

"Bound for Oklahoma, The biggest oil and gas field in the world" proclaimed the banners on the *City of Missouri* as it pulled away from Van Buren in around 1910 headed up the Arkansas River into nearby Oklahoma, which until 1906 statehood had been designated Indian Territory.

Van Buren, ca. 1910. The Crawford County Bank, with its balcony, still stands today, proudly restored on the town's historic Main Street. The city was named for the eighth president of the United States, Martin Van Buren.

15103. Court House, Ozark, Ark.; Pub. by Eugene Hall, Ozark, Ark.

Franklin County, named in 1837 for Benjamin Franklin, is one of several Arkansas counties having two courthouses: this one photographed in 1912 in the town of Ozark, the other being in Charleston. Having two county seats was deemed necessary whenever any part of the county was more than a day's wagon ride from the county seat. The Ozark courthouse, built originally in 1904, was gutted in a 1944 fire but was rebuilt. It has been said that the witnesses' view from their chair in the second-story courtroom is the most spectacular of any in Arkansas, looking out at a panoramic scene of the Ozark Mountains.

Looking North West from Court House, Ozark, Ark.

The 1910 postcard carries a view looking north west from the Franklin County Courthouse tower, over J. F. Maxey's Hardware store and Bells Confectionery. It carried the words "We have been busy packing apples. We had sixteen barrels. A man bought them by the barrel ... and we have been picking cotton too."

Booneville, September 1, 1910. The crowds turned out to hear Gov. George Donaghey dedicate the state's new Tuberculosis Sanitarium, constructed on 974 acres at a cost of fifty-thousand dollars. One of Donaghey's sisters had died of the dreaded communicable disease, which terrified people in the era before antibiotic treatments would largely eradicate it and make sanitariums obsolete. Today the site is home to a state facility for the developmentally disabled.

These two new five room Residences upon your own terms in the best residential section of the Prosperous City of Booneville, Ark. Inquire or write the Booneville, (Ark.) Realty Co.

Real estate promotions have long been a fixture of American economic life, and turn-of-the-century Arkansas was no exception. Around 1910 the Booneville Realty Company used postcards to market these two new, virtually identical homes, complete with picket fences.

Paris, ca. 1910. "Hello Kid . . . You be sure and come Xmas and bring Ethel with you," were the words carried to Van Buren. Paris, apparently named for the French capital, shares Logan County seat honors with Booneville. The buildings located on the courthouse square included P. A. Hanh and Company Drugs and School Books and the Smith Hardware Company

Magazine, ca. 1910. Among the state's more unusually named towns, this Logan County village is seen in the shadow of a mountain that was originally named by French hunters, from their word *magasin*, meaning warehouse or barn. Today the mountain is an undeveloped state park.

Subiaco, ca. 1910. The Little Rock and Fort Smith Railroad owned thousands of acres of land in the Arkansas River Valley in the 1870s. To find a market for it, the company helped arrange passage for thousands of Catholics, especially from Germany, to New York and then by train to Arkansas, where the railroad sold the immigrants farmland for as little as fifty cents an acre. To further attract the Catholic settlers, the railroad company assisted the Benedictine order in erecting a massive European-style monastery on a hill overlooking what is now the town of Subiaco (misspelled on this card). This helped ensure that there were priests to serve the area. The card's message mailed to Connecticut reads, "The card you sent was lovely. May I ask if you are Catholic. I am and I live out in the wilds of western Nebr. and do not get to go to church very often." Part of the abbey was destroyed by fire in the 1920s but was rebuilt and remains today as a boy's boarding school and a renowned retreat center still operated by the monks of St. Bendedict.

Clarksville, ca. 1912. This wagon load of peach baskets bound for the orchards was photographed before the Johnson County Courthouse (now gone). Johnson county remains noted for its peach production but today uses boxes and trucks to move its produce.

"*GO SLOW* $5 fine to drive faster than a walk over this bridge," warns the sign on the bridge crossing Spadra Creek at Clarksville. The approaching wagon of peach baskets would have been a potential violator, but the driver seems to have stopped, perhaps swayed by what would have been a large fine intended to protect the iron bridge.

Danville, ca. 1910. "Papa we will ship four cars of cattle Monday 22 at about twelve o'clock," states the message on the reverse of the card of three Yell County anglers and the catch they claimed was but an hour's work.

Dardanelle, ca. 1915. Several theories exist in state history about how the Yell County seat was named; one says it was named for the Cherokee Indian word, *dardonnie* meaning to "sleep with one eye open." This happy group of motorists, sipping their drinks through straws, had both eyes open; they seem to have been served by an early "car hop" on the right.

This card of a wagon-lined Front Street of Dardanelle, with Singer and Nolan Drugs seen on the left, was mailed by people who actually lived on the street beneath the trees in the distance. "Lois and I went down one night by ourself Will had taken Floyd to the barber shop Floyd came home while we was getting ready I sent him back we went to the theatre." Apparently Floyd was a child who resisted getting a haircut.

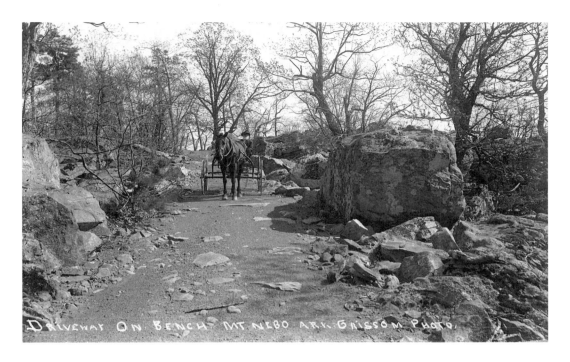

Mt. Nebo, ca. 1910. Early in the century the top of Mt. Nebo was a summer resort complete with a hotel, reached by this rocky wagon road. The hotel burned, but today a paved road leads thousands of visitors a year to Mt. Nebo State Park along the path once traveled by this plodding one-horse rig.

"Am working on a bridge gang," reads the 1917 message on the back of a postcard showing a mine with a four-hundred-foot-deep shaft, noted as the deepest in the state, of the Southern Anthracite Coal Company. Coal mining was once a significant industry in Russellville, where the photograph on this card was taken. The mine is long gone; the site is the location of a shopping area today.

Russellville, ca. 1909. The longest pontoon bridge in the world, a two-thousand-foot span, connected Russellville to Dardanelle. Originally built for wagons, the bridge was frequently damaged by floods but would serve until the 1920s when a new highway bridge was erected.

Russellville, ca. 1911. The street was cluttered with cotton wagons, their loads apparently worth fifteen cents per pound at the time. "You don't know how much I would like to be there with you. The pictures are *so cute,* and you must have enjoyed taking them," states the message exchanged between two women. Cotton was a major crop in the river valley during the first decades of the century; these bales would have been shipped by rail, in all likelihood.

Morrilton, ca. 1925. The railroad tracks and depot are out of sight on the right, across from automobile-lined Railroad Avenue. The town was established around a rail station in the 1870s and named for two brothers who laid out the town: E. J. and George Morrill. Most of the buildings still stand, but much of the business has relocated along Interstate 40.

"Hows you making it?" reads the message from the Conway County town of Plummerville sent to the freight agent at Perry, Arkansas. "Any jobs open over there, how about Havana [Yell County town]?" The well-dressed men may have posed before boarding the train at the Plummerville depot.

CENTRAL ARKANSAS

Faulkner, Grant, Lonoke, Perry, Pulaski, and Saline Counties

In the first two decades of the twentieth century, central Arkansas, with Little Rock at its heart, produced more postcards than any other part of the state except Hot Springs, which was in the heyday of its bathhouse fame.

The capital city of Little Rock, seat of government and served by two railroads, had its capitol building, Main Street, all its schools, and a score of churches all put on postcards. Cards were sold in the drugstores along Main Street, in the train depots, and by local photographers who put such things as the 1911 United Confederate Veterans' Reunion and the aftermath of fires onto their postcards.

Perhaps nothing is as telling about the passage of time and changing lifestyles as the evolution of Little Rock's Main Street as seen on postcards. The transition from wagons, to street cars, to automobiles is documented, as well as a full ten blocks lined with businesses in an era when the city limits extended only a little beyond the capitol building, and the terms "shopping center" and "mall" had not yet been coined.

Outlying farming communities like Lonoke and Sheridan were less than an hour away from Little Rock by train, but postcard images show a much more rustic way of life: dirt main streets, small frame churches, and farmers at work in their fields.

Saline County boasted its developing bauxite mines and the classic courthouse that still stands today. Postcards from remote Perry County seem only to have recorded its sawmill industry. Faulkner County, however, produced many cards of Hendrix College, a bustling business district, and a courthouse constructed by George Donaghey, the contractor who would become governor and be the driving force behind a new state capitol building.

A cluster of "Little Rock Belles" surrounded the new state capitol under construction in 1905 when this message was sent: "Sorry that you wasn't at the picnic Thursday. Be sure and go to the W.O.W. [Woodmen of the World] picnic at Hill's Lake Wednesday." The rendering of the building shows the original design of the dome, which is different from the final version.

"I spent one day attending the teachers' assn.," reads the 1911 message penned on the back of a view of the new state capitol, which was bannered for the education meeting. That year the state legislature would have its first meeting in the building modeled on the nation's capitol, but the building would not be completed until 1914, following years of controversy about the need for it, the cost, construction scandals, and defective workmanship.

Around 1910 a photographer perched on the dome of the new state capitol and pointed his camera toward downtown Little Rock, with Capitol Avenue centered in his lens. Only wagons and streetcars were in evidence, and the skyline was modest by today's standards. Virtually all the large homes seen here are long gone, replaced by commercial buildings.

This 1905 card is a view of what is today called the Old State House, which had been commissioned by Arkansas's territorial governor, John Pope, who charged that the design should, "Command the admiration and respect of the passing stranger and have a moral, and a political influence on the whole community." Opened in 1836, it served as the seat of Arkansas government until the opening of the present capitol in 1911 and is today a state-operated museum.

The German Romanesque Revival–style Pulaski County Courthouse, seen here around 1905, had been erected in 1889 at a cost of $100,000. Many changes would affect the building over the years: an annex would be put on the north side in 1912 and storm damage would necessitate the removal of the clock tower in the 1960s. The tower was replaced in 1995, and the proudly restored building still serves today.

"Dear unknown friend:" begins the 1913 message to an address in Maine, "received your card think it a beautiful scene." Built in 1881 of Ohio-quarried sandstone, the building depicted on the card served as Little Rock's post office and federal building until the construction of a new federal building in 1932; the old structure today is part of the University of Arkansas Law School.

The "little rock" after which the state's capital city was named appeared on postcards by 1910. The French explorer Bernard de La Harpe had searched for a fabled giant green rock in 1722, hoping to find an emerald. Instead he found this rock at the first upland site he came to as he ascended the Arkansas River. Overgrown and neglected for years, the site was cleaned up and made accessible to visitors as part of Little Rock's river front redevelopment in recent years.

This card, mailed in 1906 to Wales and actually printed in and imported from England, pictured strollers in Little Rock's City Park. The building had been built in 1842 as a military arsenal, changed hands three times during the Civil War, and was the site of the birth of World War II hero Gen. Douglas MacArthur in 1880. The park today bears his name, and the building serves as a museum.

The original Arkansas School for the Blind was opened by a blind Baptist minister at Arkadelphia in 1858. In 1870 the school was moved to Little Rock, where this building was erected on Center Street. In 1916 the school proudly added a dictaphone to be used by the superintendent, with his letters then to be typed by the students of the school. The building was taken down to allow construction of the Governor's Mansion in the 1950s, with the bricks being incorporated into the governor's new house.

In 1867 Joseph Mount, a deaf man who had been trained at the Pennsylvania Institute for the Deaf, opened a school in Little Rock for children with impaired hearing. In 1868 the state took over the facility, naming it the Arkansas Deaf Mute Institute. The school, shown here around 1910, went on to attain national recognition and still serves today as the Arkansas School for the Deaf.

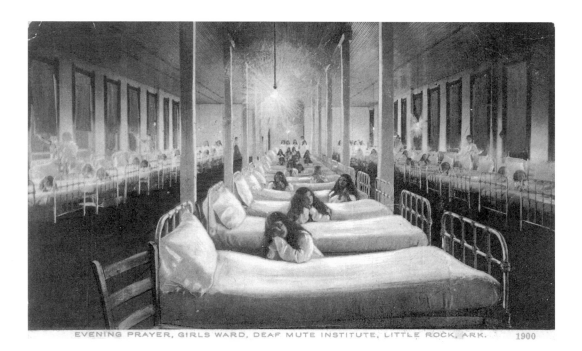

EVENING PRAYER, GIRLS WARD, DEAF MUTE INSTITUTE, LITTLE ROCK, ARK.   1900

This 1912 card shows the residents of the girl's ward of the Deaf Mute Institute saying their evening prayers in the huge open ward. The card would likely have tugged on the heart strings of those who found it in their mail box.

ARKANSAS REFORM SCHOOL, LITTLE ROCK, ARK.

The Arkansas Reform School was located four miles west of Little Rock, having been erected in 1905 at a cost of thirty-thousand dollars for both the land and the building. The annual salary for the superintendent was set at fifteen hundred dollars. The facility's name would be changed to the Boys Industrial School in 1917, and in 1919 it would be moved to Pine Bluff to take advantage of more productive farmland.

Trolley cars were in their heyday when this 1914 card of the lower end of Little Rock's Main Street was mailed. Streetcars like the three in this photo were originally mule-drawn conveyances. These are seen passing such well-known establishments in Arkansas retailing history as Cohn's, Blass, and Houck's Music Store. To the upper left is part of the sign for Gus Blass' Dry Goods Store; the domed building is the Masonic Temple at Fifth and Main, which burned around 1920.

This 1905 view of the of the intersection of Seventh and Main found a horse-drawn wagon parked before a grocery store, the site of which is today a parking lot. Draughon's School of Business, on the right, was housed in a building constructed by George Donaghey, an area contractor who would become governor in 1909; the building still stands today.

The intersection of Capitol and Main Streets was probably the crossroads of the state at the time of this card, around 1918. Business signs include the Palace Theater, Union Dentist ("teeth extracted without pain"), Selleck's Pharmacy, and Blass Department Store. Traffic includes automobiles, a horse-drawn buggy, and a streetcar in the distance.

West Markham St. from Main St., Little Rock, Ark.

A view of West Markham Street taken from Main around 1905 reflects one of the most changed streets in Arkansas. In the distance on the right is the Hotel Marion; the entire block is today occupied by the Statehouse Convention Center and the Excelsior Hotel. The building on the left corner is long gone; however, down the street from it is the Capitol Hotel, which has been restored and is operating today.

The Hotel Marion was for many years the center of business and political activity in Little Rock. The 175-room hotel opened in 1906 and over the years played host to Theodore Roosevelt, Will Rogers, Helen Keller, and Charles Lindbergh. The 1918 message reads, "I send you this card to let you know that I was in this hotel last night, and say Ma it is sure some place believe me." The hotel was demolished in 1980 to make way for the Excelsior Hotel.

On January 3, 1911, fire did an estimated one million dollars in damage along Little Rock's Main Street. Among the casualties seen in this rare nighttime photo are the Hollenberg Music Store and the Hanley Company, which are going up in flames as the ineffective pumper truck in the foreground throws its feeble stream of water. The city's leaders used this fire as evidence of the need to upgrade the town's fire-fighting equipment.

Originally established by the Sisters of Charity of Nazareth in 1888, Saint Vincent Infirmary moved to this location at Tenth and High Streets in 1910, about the time this card was made. The facility opened the state's first training school for nurses in 1906 and later was one of the first twelve hospitals in the nation to install X-ray equipment. The building was torn down around 1960 after the hospital relocated to Markham and University Avenues, where it continues to operate today.

The main buildings of what was then called the Arkansas Insane Asylum were completed in 1882 but within six months became overcrowded as patients from private facilities, poorhouses, and jails poured in. The hospital had by necessity expanded by the time this card was mailed about 1910. Today the same site houses the very modern Arkansas State Hospital.

During the early years of this century, the state's medical school operated near what is now MacArthur Park; it was most likely there that a group of medical students posed with a medical bag and a skeleton. It can be inferred from this 1908 photo that medical students' unique sense of humor is nothing new.

Snodgrass and Bracy's Rexall Drug Store was located in the one-hundredth block of Main Street in Little Rock and made some bold claims on this 1910 card. At the bottom of the card it says "We never close," and one of the pennants suspended from the ceiling reads "Open All Night—This Store Hasn't Closed Once in 14 Years."

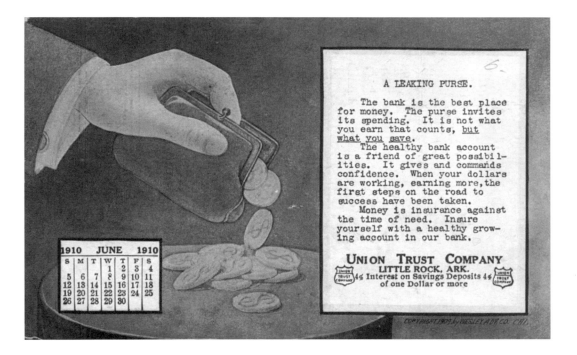

Little Rock was the state's center for banking at the time of this card, in 1910, and one financial institution, Union Trust Company, sought deposits by means of this postcard motto: "It is not what you earn that counts, *but what you save.*" The institution offered 4 percent interest on deposits of one dollar or more. The calendar would have encouraged potential customers to keep the card visible for the entire month of June.

The Majestic Theater was located in the eight-hundredth block of Little Rock's Main Street and in this 1905 view displayed signs advertising, "Matinee at 2:00." The playhouse offered some of the finer musical comedies in the state and hosted Will Rogers in the 1920s. The building would burn in 1930. Today the site is a parking lot.

The Peabody School, built in the 1890s, was reportedly Little Rock's first brick school building. It was located at Fifth and Gaines and displayed its imposing presence to streetcars passing between downtown and the state capitol building. The school would be torn down in the 1950s; the site is now home to the Federal Building.

A DRESS MAKING CLASS TAUGHT BY MISS EVA BUTTON IN LITTLE ROCK, ARK.
WOMEN'S BAPTIST HOME MISSION SOCIETY, CHICAGO, ILL.

In Little Rock, as in the entire South, segregated education was the rule during the first half of the century and certainly so when this 1910 card was mailed to Bohemia with the message written in German. The discussion that ensued can only be imagined when the card arrived in Europe from Little Rock showing Miss Eva Button teaching young black girls to sew.

"Gus Ottenheimer Football Team. Nov. 15th, 1908 Gus O. Mgr.," reads the back of this Little Rock card of a group of wide-eyed boys in football formation. Gus, most likely behind the center, would grow up to own and operate a clothing manufacturing plant in Little Rock and would ship its products worldwide.

The 1908 message on the back of this view of the Little Rock High School's girl's basketball team reads, "What do you think about this picture? Isn't it queer looking? Gee! but you seem to be in an awful big hurry to answer that letter. Am beginning to think something is about to happen. Eve hasn't heard nor I either. Get busy quick."

Little Rock, ca. 1910. Homes went up rapidly as Little Rock grew around the new capitol and beyond. This home was under construction at 1424 West Fourth, with workmen standing on seemingly rickety scaffolding. The product of these men's hard work would be torn down in the late 1960s.

"Heres where you get a good babsousing," reads this 1908 card, complete with the sender's art work on a view of the handsome new sanctuary of the Second Baptist Church. The building was torn down in the 1950s; the site today is occupied by the classroom building for the church, whose sanctuary is now housed in a new, adjacent building.

Temple B'nai Israel was organized in 1866 by a group of Jewish Civil War veterans. The temple, pictured here in 1907, was completed in 1872 at a cost of seven thousand dollars. It was torn down in 1972 to make way for the First Commercial Bank tower. The congregation relocated to western Little Rock.

15507—Temple B'nei' Israel, Little Rock, Ark.

Jewish church on fifth & Broadway.

Orphanages have faded into history for the most part, but during the first half of the century St. Joseph's Orphanage near North Little Rock was home to hundreds of children. The 1910 message reads, "How are you? I am about to roast and having lots of rain too. Weeds are higher than the cotton and snakes to let and James is tired of his motor cycle and is going to send it back."

In May of 1911 Little Rock was adorned as the city hosted the United Confederate Veterans' Reunion, part of which is seen here near the event headquarters, the Hotel Marion. During that week the city's population of 45,000 swelled to 150,000, including more than 10,000 old rebel soldiers. Many spectators came for one of the last chances to see such a large gathering of the men who had marched off to war fifty years before.

The unexpectedly large number of Confederate veterans prompted creation of a tent city in the Little Rock City Park, using eleven hundred army tents loaned by nearby Fort Roots. The city kept its pledge to house and feed the old soldiers, who came with an appetite: in three days they consumed 16,000 loaves of bread, 8,000 pounds of steak, 3,000 pounds of roast beef, 110 cases of eggs, 350 bushels of potatoes, and 1,700 pounds of coffee. The tent camp was named for "Fighting Bob" Shaver, the designated camp commander, who had led the Twenty-seventh Arkansas Regiment during the war.

The United Confederate Veterans' Reunion concluded with a parade through Little Rock; more than 100,000 people lined the streets to watch the aging soldiers pass. The veterans were accompanied by fourteen bands playing "Dixie," floats, the survivors of General Nathan Bedford Forrest's mounted cavalry, and an assortment of bullet-riddled, frayed battle flags preserved since the Appomattox surrender some forty-six years before. It would be one of the last times such a group would assemble; the "thin gray line" would dwindle rapidly in the years following the reunion. A bugler played taps at the depot as the old soldiers boarded trains for their trips home, the day after the reunion parade.

MISSOURI PACIFIC-IRON MOUNTAIN STATION AT LITTLE ROCK, ARKANSAS

Little Rock was served by two train stations, the larger of which was the Union Station of the Missouri Pacific–Iron Mountain Railroad. The large, covered area to the right is for passenger loading. The station was erected between 1906 and 1909 in an Italian-influenced design with its many arched windows and the clock tower. In 1920 the station was destroyed by fire, and the replacement was built in a similar, though flat-roofed style. It is still in use today for the infrequent stops of Amtrak trains.

The Argenta (today North Little Rock) rail yards were massive, with a broad section of switches to route the many trains per day. This 1910 postcard bore the message "This is where so many men get killed," vivid testimony to the dangers of working for the railroads of the era.

A 1910 card of the Missouri Pacific roundhouse shows the service center where maintenance and repairs were done on the locomotives. Multiple engines could be backed into this structure, allowing workmen to reach the undersides from the pits below the tracks.

Argenta, ca. 1915. The city known since 1917 as North Little Rock has carried many names, including DeCantillon, Hunterville, Baring Cross, and Quapaw. The town was named Argenta in 1866 because of silver ore deposits found in the area, though these were not of commercial quality. This card shows the city's Main Street, with Union Furniture Store on the right and a liquor store on the left corner.

This ca. 1880 army post overlooking the Arkansas River was named for Logan H. Roots, a Union veteran of the Civil War and a prominent local businessman who helped secure the fort for Arkansas. Today the facility, with many original buildings, such as the one seen in this 1907 view, serves as a Veterans Administration hospital.

RECRUITS AT DRILL, CAMP PIKE, LITTLE ROCK, ARK.

The coming of World War I created an immediate need for army training bases. A civic effort in North Little Rock bought thousands of acres of land, which were given to the federal government to build Camp Pike, named for frontier explorer Zebulon Pike. Pictured on this card are newly-arrived draftees, still in civilian clothing, in front of the barracks. The camp, built to house sixty-five thousand troops, contained two thousand buildings, required forty million board feet of lumber to construct, and had a weekly payroll of $300,000, an important consideration for the city that secured the base.

Among the business enterprises setting up near Camp Pike during World War I was the photography studio that captured these two young soldiers posing with pistols drawn and with Old Glory as a backdrop. Such cards would have been mailed home. The soldiers would board a train upon completion of their training and begin the long journey to the war in France.

World War I brought new technology to the battlefield, therefore requiring training new skills. Camp Pike, with this "aero mechanics" class, did its part. Notable is the racially-integrated class in a photo taken many years before segregation would be banned in the armed forces.

Women did their part at the sprawling Camp Pike army training camp, as evidenced by this group of nurses outside the base hospital. The women, in casual dress and astride army mounts, are preparing to enjoy a horseback ride.

Logging in western Pulaski County was a major industry early in the century, and many small sawmills like this converted trees to lumber. The prominent peak in the background is Pinnacle Mountain, today a popular state park.

"Please send me a postal card in return of any view," reads the 1906 message on this card of the Saline County Courthouse located in Benton. The courthouse, constructed of yellow brick, was erected in 1902 and still serves today.

A popular vantage point for early postcard photos was the local courthouse tower, this one shot from atop Saline County's. The 1907 message observes, "You would think that there was something to Benton judging from this picture wouldn't you?"

Benton, ca. 1911. Bush's Drugstore is typical of such stores of the era, with a classic soda fountain to the left, a glass case of cigars to the right, ceiling fans, and a high embossed-tin ceiling.

Bauxite, ca. 1910. Vast deposits of bauxite (aluminum ore) were discovered in Saline County in the 1890s. The American Bauxite Mine is shown here, where these hard-working men are apparently laying a short rail line used to remove the ore extracted from strip mines. The bauxite industry would be the backbone of the local economy for many years, until the mines played out in the 1980s.

Benton, ca. 1910. Valuable clay deposits in the area supported two potteries, which distributed products nationwide. A youngster dressed in overalls poses with some of the wares; the message reads, "Don't you think this is a cute picture?"

The small Saline County village of Alexander, with church steeples and smoking chimneys prominent, was most likely photographed from a water tower for this 1913 card. The message sent to Oklahoma from Alexander is "I have a nice collection of cards. . . . so I wish to exchange with you as I have not got a card from your state."

The message on this card from Conway in 1908 reads, "Mr. Donaghey sends his regards." George W. Donaghey as a struggling building contractor had rebuilt the Faulkner County Courthouse following a fire in the 1890s. He would be elected governor of Arkansas in 1908. Faulkner County was named for Sandford Faulkner, who is credited with authorship of the original "Arkansas Traveler" poem.

Conway, ca. 1907. A happy group posed on the shore of Gold Lake on this card with the message, "This is our . . . picnic place where you had such good luck. Can you find the good place on the card?" Today the lake is called Lake Conway and is still a prime "good luck" fishing spot.

This postcard of the busy Conway business district was used by a salesman for the postcard company to secure an order for one thousand of these cards to be delivered to Selby's 5–10 and 25 Cent Store at a total cost of $6.25, to be shipped August 7, 1925. In the distance a horse-drawn wagon can be seen among the automobiles.

Sheridan, ca. 1908. Founded during Civil War Reconstruction, the Grant County rural community was named to honor Union General Phillip Sheridan. The county itself bore the name of Sheridan's commander, General Ulysses S. Grant. Much of the small town's business district is seen here on this block of Oak Street.

"My Dear Clara," reads the 1908 message from the remote Grant County village of Leola, "This card will remind you of the 'reunion.'" Apparently this crowd moving down the dusty dirt street of the lumber community, probably representing most of its population, was involved in the reunion mentioned.

Lonoke, ca. 1908. Unique in the state, this county seat bears the same name as its county, both said to have been named for a huge red "lone" oak tree. The sign above the parked wagon is "The Best Furniture for Less Money." On the corner to the left is a water pump, which would have likely refreshed man and horse alike.

Lonoke, ca. 1910. Their wagon loaded with milk cans, a man and boy were probably heading for town. The windmill towering behind the farmhouse provided water for the farm; the barn sheltered its horses and farm tools.

Lonoke, ca. 1909. Most likely tin shop owner J. A. Robinson is standing behind the large tin pipe in front of his business. The message reads, "What are you going to do on the 3rd [of July]? I am thinking of going to Des Arc fishing and stay about a week." The tin business was important in this era, furnishing such things as tin roofs and irrigation pipes in rice fields.

5472 The House still standing in Carlisle, Arkansas, in which Opie Read, the great American humorist, established his first paper the Prairie Flower, in 1876

Carlisle, ca. 1909. Southern humorist O. P. Read established his first newspaper in this house in 1876. The paper's masthead bore the motto, "If you have to walk, be sure to start on time." The town was reportedly named by its founder, Samuel McCormick, after Carlisle, Pennsylvania, where he once lived.

Carlisle, ca. 1909. Workers were photographed loading rice, which was hauled into town by wagons and loaded onto freight cars of the Frisco Railroad for shipment. The train tracks still run directly through the center of this small farming community, which produced one of the state's first rice crops in 1904.

Cabot, ca. 1905. Today it is one of the state's fastest growing communities, but at the time of this card the northern Lonoke County community had a weed-lined, dirt Main Street. The town, according to legend, was named for an engineer on the Cairo Fulton Railroad. It had a long business section housing barber shops, a drugstore, several general stores, and a furniture store.

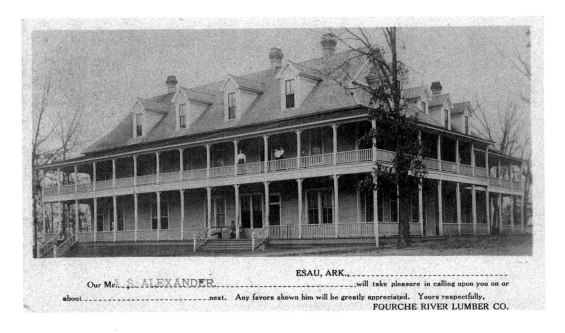

The Perry County community of Esau no longer appears on maps, but in 1908 it was one of many sawmill towns in the South. Founded by the Fourche River Lumber Company, the mill community had a hotel that was used by the company's salesmen as a base for calls on prospective customers.

Esau, ca. 1905. The mill of the Fourche River Lumber Company was reflected in the waters of the mill pond where logs were stored until pulled up the conveyor belt to the waiting saws. This card was used to notify customers of shipment of their lumber orders.

GARLAND COUNTY AND HOT SPRINGS

BASED ON TWENTY YEARS of research, the authors estimate that the resort city of Hot Springs accounted for about 20 percent of the countless thousands of postcards produced in Arkansas during the first two decades of the twentieth century. The reason was that the hot springs that had amazed the Spanish Explorer Desoto some four hundred years before eventually brought millions of people from around the nation to bathe in and drink the waters.

The belief in the curative powers of the hot mineral water was widespread, and their promotion gave rise to scores of bathhouses and grand hotels. *Hot Springs, Arkansas,* a book published in 1910 by the Missouri Pacific–Iron Mountain Railroad, declared that "In bringing before a larger and more health-eager public the advantages of Hot Springs, Ark., America's thermal wonderland, one point, and a most important one, has been persistently overlooked. It is this: The Hot Springs of Arkansas are not the most curative mass of heated water that gushes from any fissure in any part of the known world, *just because these springs are hot,* but because the waters *contain a curative agent not found anywhere on earth.*"

The testimonials of the miraculous nature of the hot waters came not only from the private sector which stood to make a profit from visitors, but also from major government officials. In *Hot Springs, Arkansas,* R. M. O'Reilly, U.S. Surgeon General and Secretary of War Elias Root, offered a letter that contained the following: "Relief may be reasonably expected at the Hot Springs in the following conditions: gout and rheumatism, neuralgia, malarial poisoning, paralysis not of organic nature, chronic Brights disease (the early stages only), diseases of the urinary organs; functional diseases of the liver; gastric dyspepsia, chronic diarrhea, chronic skin diseases, especially of squamous varieties." In the era before modern medicine with its knowledge, miracle drugs, and technology it is little wonder that millions flocked to Hot Springs, where the springs were owned and controlled by the U.S. government.

The spa city was truly at the height of its glory in the first two decades of the twentieth century. In 1910 the city boasted twenty-four bathhouses containing six hundred tubs, which often administered eight thousand baths per day, as compared with only two functioning facilities today. The visitors came in droves, usually by train, and they sent postcards around the world in the millions.

The bathhouses, while privately operated, were strictly regulated by the U.S. government, which set the prices for both baths and attendants' fees. A partial listing of the bathhouses, all of which graced postcards, included the Arlington, Alhambra, Great Northern, Magnesia, Majestic, Rockafellow, Lamar, Maurice, and the Horse Shoe, named for its horseshoe-shaped windows. These bathing facilities were restricted to white patrons, while a separate house, the Pythian Sanitarium, was established for black visitors.

The advertised prices of the baths were governed by the opulence, or lack of it, in the respective bathhouses. Single baths at the Arlington were fifty-five cents or ten dollars for a course of twenty-one baths, ranging downward to thirty-five cents per bath at the Ozark.

In that bathing was a government-controlled industry, there was even provision for the impoverished: a "government free bathhouse" was operated for the indigent, who could soak at no charge.

The baths not only brought people to Hot Springs but also apparently kept them there for extended stays. In the book *Hot Springs, Arkansas,* the author made a case for how inexpensively a bather could stay for a month at a time by detailing a forty-six-dollar-per-month budget as follows:

Board and lodging	$15 to $90
Physician's fees	$20 to $30
Medicine (if needed)	$5 to $10
Bathing	$3 to $5
Bath Attendants (if needed)	$3 to $5
Total	$46 to $145

The messages taken from the backs of some of the postcards mailed from Hot Springs give first hand accounts of the impressions of visitors and hint at their length of stay. A 1910 message read, "I really think mother is getting better and if she stays another month to take the baths she should be cured." A 1911 card declared, "I am taking the baths and feeling much better already, $13 for 21 baths." A man named Herb wrote in 1909, "I got hare all wright at 9-30. Doctor Willens sed I would haft to stay about a month for the baths."

Another visitor in 1913 was not so enamored of the waters, "Dear son and Mama, send me at once about 1 dozen of your liver tablets. This hot water is very constipating. Love and kisses, Papa."

Hotels, grand and plain, rose to cater to the thousands of visitors. Most of these are now long gone, victims of fire, time, and simple short-sightedness about saving our historical heritage. However virtually all the lodging places, towering hotels, and humble boarding houses, were captured on postcards for the benefit of visitors and as a form of advertising the accommodations and room rates printed on the cards.

The grandest hotel was likely the Arlington, which contained three hundred rooms and was constructed in 1893 at a cost of $550,000. The frontage stretched 650 feet with a brick, stone, and iron verandah. Tucked into the base of Hot Springs Mountain, the twin-towered Moorish-style hotel operated year round and quoted rates of $4 to $8 per day in 1910. The hotel was destroyed by fire in 1923, to be rebuilt as the Arlington modern-day visitors today know.

The other grand hotel in Hot Springs was the Eastman, with five hundred rooms, and rates comparable to the Arlington. Some of Hot Springs' wealthiest visitors chose the Eastman for their sojourns to the resort city. A visitor named Lulu wrote in 1910, "Many people of wealth are here from Chicago and New York. Uncle Billy went to the horse show ball at the Eastman Hotel with an ex-wife of a millionaire. Andrew Carnegie and young Jay Gould were at the hotel and dancing till all hours." The hotel declined with the deterioration of the bathing industry, became part of the Army and Navy Hospital that served the wounded soldiers sent home from the battlefields of World War II, and ultimately was demolished in the 1950s.

The only other large hotels in the spa city were the Majestic and the Park, but a host of smaller hotels also served visitors. Those with a capacity of one hundred to two hundred guests included the Great Northern, the Milwaukee, the Moody, the St. Charles, the Eddy, and the Waukesha. Smaller hotels with capacities of fifty to one hundred included the Colonial, Hotel Richmond, the Rockafellow, and the Goddard, most of which offered lodging with rates beginning at one dollar per day. Almost all these buildings are gone today, and only the Majestic and the rebuilt Park continue to operate.

There was a diverse amusement industry that sprang up to cater to visitors when they were not soaking in the hot mineral waters. Oaklawn Park began its horse racing tradition, taking over from Essex Park, which ran horses at the fairgrounds shortly after the century began. Horseback riding along mountainside trails was promoted by riding stables located behind the Arlington Hotel. Streetcars would speed visitors up Central Avenue to other attractions along Whittington and Park Avenues.

The Alligator Farm, still in business today, entertained visitors as did the nearby Ostrich Farm which seemed to appeal especially to visiting ladies. In one account a woman admired the plumes on one of the great birds and remarked, "Oh, how I wish I might pluck one of those beautiful feathers." An attendant replied, "All right, lady; I will give you as many as you will pull." It was a safe offer because few would approach these birds that weighed close to four hundred pounds. The feathers that the birds molted were sold in the farm's gift shop until the facility closed in the 1940s.

The images on postcards paint Hot Springs in the first decades of the twentieth century as a magical, world-class resort. It existed in a time that is long past and is best remembered through the postcards actually held in the hands of the believers who came to partake of the curative hot waters that bubbled from the earth.

Central Ave., ca. 1900. The photographer captured the spa city's most renowned thoroughfare lined with business enterprises. Note two sets of streetcar tracks: cars went both ways. The movement of the horse caused it to blur as it passed the New Oklahoman Furnished Rooms, which also housed a business advertising "Clairvoyants."

10388. GOVERNMENT RESERVATION BATH HOUSE ROW, HOT SPRINGS, ARK.

"Government Reservation Bath House Row," reads this ca. 1900 view likely taken from one of the towers of the Arlington Hotel. Six streetcars are in view passing the fabled turn-of-the-century bathhouses which include, left to right, the Superior, the Hale, the Maurice, and the Palace—all of which have been replaced by later versions. On the hill the Army and Navy Hospital is visible to the left, and to the right the pointed observation tower of the Eastman Hotel rises.

Imperial Bath House, ca. 1910. The ornateness of some of the long-gone bathhouses can only be imagined from cards such as this. The Imperial sat below the Army and Navy Hospital and charged fifty cents for a bath or ten dollars for a course of twenty-one baths. Today the building is gone, and a National Park Administration building occupies the site.

Maurice Bath House, ca. 1915. William G. Maurice, a St. Louis native, began visiting Hot Springs in 1870 at the age of eleven, accompanying his mother. He returned in 1890 to build the first Maurice Bath House and replaced it with this handsome marble facility in 1912. The facility was billed as "the most complete sanitary bathing establishment in the world."

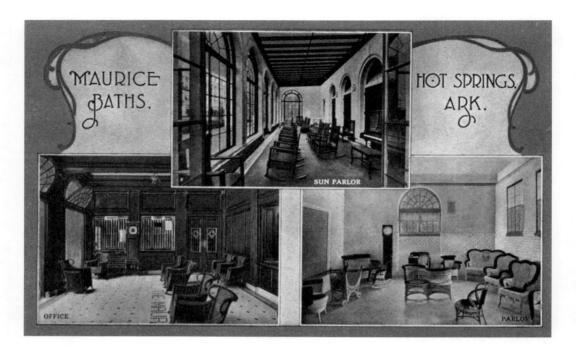

Maurice Bath House, ca. 1915. Pictured are the sun parlor (top), the office (left), and the bath parlor. The facility advertised special treatments such as those conducted by F. F. Hellwig of Moscow, Russia, who did electromassage treatments, and by Mrs. Charlotte Hedwig of Sweden, a masseuse practicing "original Swedish movements," all with "no muscle jerking or nerve-wracking sensations."

Maurice Bath House, ca. 1915. The spa boasted this bath lounge room, and its bathing department featured marble tubs. According to the back of the card, the billiard room had "Art glass windows, tile wainscoting and painted frieze, 'The Chase' by Frederick Warnecke." The bathing lounge had similar features, including a forty by forty foot skylight. A bath at the Maurice cost fifty cents. Today the building stands idle, awaiting restoration.

This 1916 view was taken behind the Maurice Bath House where visitors lined up on a cold day to drink from the hot spring that bubbled up and served as a drinking fountain at the Maurice spring.

The magnificent Spanish Renaissance–design Arlington Hotel and Bath House opened with three hundred rooms in 1893, constructed at a cost of $550,000. Built on the site of the first Arlington Hotel of 1875, it boasted a verandah running 650 feet along Central and Fountain Avenues. This card was produced around 1910 when a room would have cost between four and eight dollars per day.

A Cleveland, Ohio, visitor in 1913 sent home a view of the Arlington's wicker-adorned sun parlor, a popular winter feature with hotel guests. The hotel provided wheelchairs in which invalid guests could be taken to the adjacent bathhouse, to the sun room, and even to one of three daily concerts by the hotel's own orchestra.

On a warm April afternoon in 1923 famed detective William Pinkerton was among the guests seated on the Arlington's veranda when smoke was reported coming from the hotel's basement. Initially considered minor, the fire would prove a disaster; the ambulance pictured would be joined by the city's fire fighters and hordes of gawkers.

The 1923 fire would completely destroy the thirty-year-old Arlington Hotel. The tragedy included the death of one fireman, George Ford, a father of seven who was crushed beneath a falling wall. There were many reports of dramatic rescues from windows by fireman and volunteers. The hotel would be rebuilt by 1930 and still operates today.

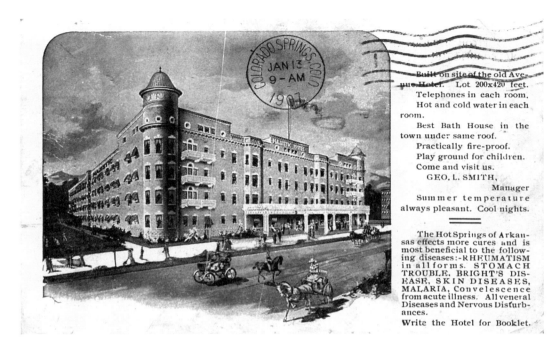

The Majestic Hotel was built in 1902 near the intersection of Park, Whittington, and Central Avenues, where it still serves visitors today. Each floor had access to the mountain side. Rates were quoted at $2.50 per day around the 1907 date this card was mailed.

In 1916 the Majestic Hotel's waiters posed at the rear of the hotel. In an era when few public spa facilities were open to black clientele, it is ironic how dependent the industry was on these men.

When completed in 1890 the Eastman Hotel was the largest in Hot Springs, and perhaps in the nation, with 520 guest rooms. From its opening day it carried the title "The Monarch of the Glen." A stay cost four dollars to eight dollars per day around the 1908 date of this card.

The Eastman Hotel catered to some of the wealthiest visitors to Hot Springs, and some took advantage of such transportation as is pictured here in front of the elegant hotel. Such reported visitors as the younger Jay Gould were welcomed in a magnificent lobby beneath crystal chandeliers.

The Eastman's observation tower rose some two hundred feet above the landscaped hotel grounds and offered such views as the one shown here. The tower was removed in the 1930s, and the hotel was converted to an Army and Navy Hospital annex in World War II. It was torn down in the 1950s to make way for a post office.

Not all the city's lodging was on a grand scale: numerous small hotels and boarding houses dotted the area. One of these was the Knickerbocker Hotel on Prospect Avenue. In the local paper the hotel touted itself as a "House of welcome, freedom and convenience, comfort and fellowship."

The Park Hotel was erected on Malvern Avenue in 1890, some distance from the other downtown hotels; its three hundred rooms were surrounded by broad, landscaped grounds. At the top of the hotel was an observatory-sunroom, all sides of which were glass. A thermal bathhouse was connected to the hotel.

"Dear Mama: The reverse will show you all that remains of the Park Hotel—the best hotel in our city." This grand hotel had been lost in 1913 in the worst fire in Hot Springs' history when a reported fifty square blocks went up in the inferno.

THE ROCKAFELLOW HOTEL AND BATH HOUSE, HOT SPRINGS, ARK.

Charles Rockafellow had come to Hot Springs in 1866 to establish the city's first drugstore. In 1901 he erected this hotel and bathhouse at the corner of Central and Park Avenues. The card promotes the egg-boiling properties of the facility's spring. The hotel was torn down in the 1960s.

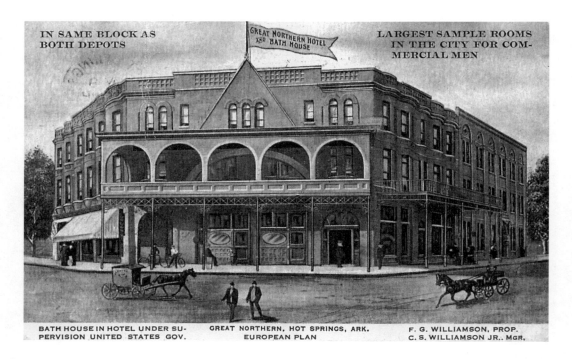

The Great Northern Hotel, built around 1900 near the rail depots, catered to the traveling businessman with room rates starting at around two dollars per day. The hotel went up in flames with at least one fatality in 1947, when a drunken guest went to sleep with a lighted cigarette.

The Horse Shoe Bath House was among several wooden frame bathing establishments that lined Central Avenue at the turn of the century. This ca. 1910 card shows the distinctive windows and advertised twenty-one baths for four dollars. The bathhouse was torn down in the 1920s and replaced by the Quapaw, which still stands.

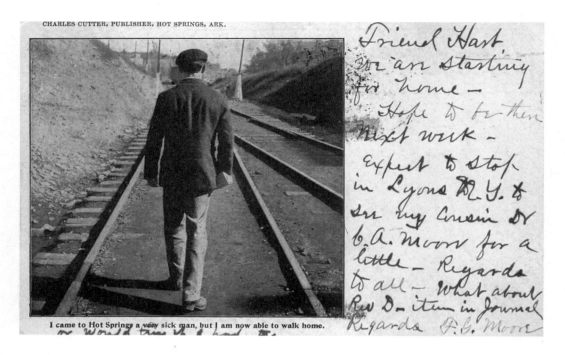

A New York visitor in 1909 penned, "I am starting for home" on a card with the declaration "I came to Hot Springs a very sick man, but I am now able to walk home." Though tongue in cheek, the card also reflected the widespread belief in the healing power of the spa waters.

Water in Hot Springs wasn't always a blessing: periodically, floods roared through the central business district. These rain-slickered men and their horse paused for the postcard photographer in the aftermath of a 1910 torrent.

Perhaps the worst of floods in the spa city's history occurred in 1923. The local newspaper reported "hundreds of thrilling rescues" when "a stream of 9 feet of water coursed madly through the valley." The rains were over but the waters were yet to recede from Central Avenue, when this photo was taken.

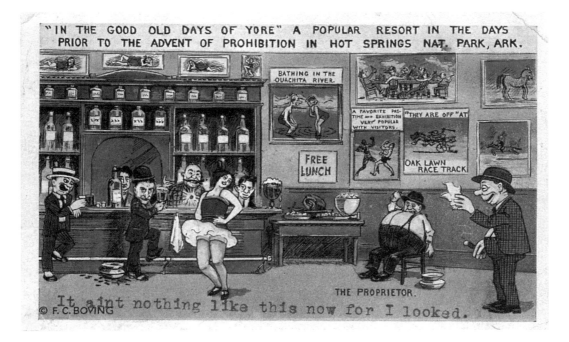

When prohibition came to Arkansas in 1915, it was perhaps most felt in the resort city of Hot Springs; however, it did generate postcard humor as in this remembrance of how the city looked before going dry.

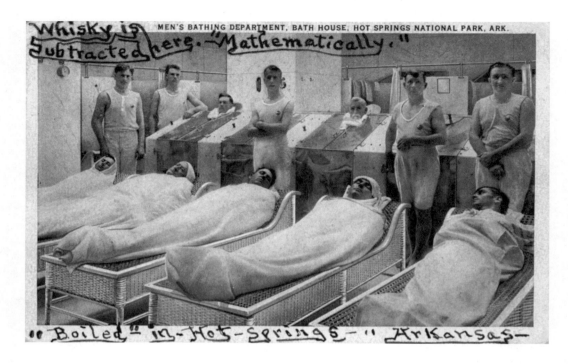

One visitor around 1920 poked fun at what might have referred to a disregard of prohibition, "Whisky is subtracted mathematically." The bathhouse was probably the Maurice.

During prohibition the Happy Hollow photo studio, located behind the Arlington Hotel, erected a prop saloon where countless visitors posed pretending to consume alcohol. The signs carried such quips as "Don't kick about the drinks. You might be weak some day yourself."

The Happy Hollow amusement park, zoo, shooting gallery, and photography studio opened around 1900. Until it closed in 1948, it would produce postcards of visitors posed with a wide variety of props, including the stuffed alligator seen with these men around 1910.

The Texas Bridge Company constructed this 165-foot observation tower at a cost of twenty thousand dollars in 1906 on Hot Springs Mountain, with a permit from the U.S. government. The views were spectacular and thousands of tourists visited the attraction during its long life. It was removed in 1971 and replaced by a new tower.

7444. Driving Alligator at Alligator Farm, Hot Springs, Ark.

In 1902 H. I. Campbell started a live alligator farm with fifty reptiles imported from the Florida Everglades. The farm quickly became a popular tourist draw, even for very young tourists like the one shown in his mother's arms.

The alligator farm, located on the streetcar line on Whittington Avenue, offered some unique photo opportunities, such as the chance to send home a card of yourself atop what, we can only assume, was a deceased and stuffed resident of the farm. The largest reptile on exhibit reportedly weighed nine hundred pounds and was named Pine Bluff after the site of his capture.

In 1900 Thomas Cockburn brought in three hundred ostriches and established a popular tourist attraction on his Whittington Avenue property. The largest of the big birds weighed 375 pounds and often did stunts like pulling a plow. The ostrich farm would operate until 1953.

Race Track Pavilion, Hot Springs, Ark.

A $500,000 investment from forty men formed the Oaklawn Jockey Club and horse-racing track in 1904. During the first season there were no parimutuel windows, and the betting was handled by bookies who rented booths from the track for one hundred dollars per day. The track continues to operate today.

Perhaps a northern visitor captured some "Ozark Hillbillies" in this 1923 photo, their wagon surrounded at a Central Avenue intersection. The occupants of the vehicles seem to have been using the fountain in the street.

The Central Methodist Church, with its stone arches and stained glass windows, was erected in 1907 to replace a church that had burned in the fire of 1905. The sign at the left of the door reads "Needle Work Guild, Walk in."

On September 5, 1913, a laundress left a charcoal burner near some shirts, and the resulting fire was the worst in the city's history. For a time containment looked possible, and the crowds gathered to watch the inferno at what seemed a safe distance behind the Central Methodist Church.

Fifty square blocks were destroyed in the 1913 fire that did ten million dollars in damages; obliterated were the rail station, the high school, and the Central Methodist Church, its once massive stone works and graceful stained glass reduced to a smoky ruin with the dawn.

THEN AND NOW

A NATURAL RESPONSE when looking at picture postcards from some four generations ago is to wonder "How different does that street look today?" or "I wonder if that building is still there?" The following pages offer an attempt to answer some of those musings because we have had the same thoughts and questions ourselves. In traveling the state for business or on family outings, we have often found ourselves with camera in one hand and postcards in the other, looking for a familiar façade.

The experience of standing on an Arkansas city street in the 1990s, with a photo of the same locale from eighty or more years ago, is one we would highly recommend. There is a sense of excitement and discovery when familiar roof lines are found or when careful scrutiny of windows, cornices, and other architectural details reveal a match. Like an echo from the past, or the familiar-yet-changed face of an old friend, the newly-constructed edifice so proudly displayed on the postcard begins to emerge from beneath the false fronts, tempered glass, and plastic signs the years may have added. Looking at the scenes that were once filled with electric streetcars and horse-drawn wagons, nattily dressed young men, and long-skirted women, one gets a sense of connection to those early Arkansans and their lives. History may not exactly come alive in those moments, but it does begin to stir a bit.

An even fuller sense of that connection has been found when we have wandered into a modern business establishment with a question and have been referred to an "old timer" who was happy to reminisce about the scenes depicted in our cards. Most people we queried have been gracious in sharing information, helping us find that old church or hotel we couldn't quite locate.

Perhaps half the time the building we sought, or even its whole block, was gone, the victim of a long-ago fire or demolition for a parking lot or a newer building. Fortunately, there have also been plenty of occasions when we found the street, church, or hotel and readily identified it, as in the seven examples that follow.

We hope that readers will be inspired to search out the location of some of the scenes on these postcards. The cards show Arkansas as the generation of World War I would have seen it; from our vantage point at the opposite end of the century, how do we now see our communities? The key to saving much of our home-town heritage is to encourage people to care about its preservation. It is our sincere hope that this book might play some part in that preservation.

Hazen, ca. 1910 and 1995. The building housing the local bank (center), post office (right), and C. E. Gillespie's store was completed in 1909, the year before this card (opposite) was printed. By 1995 all these concerns had long since closed, and the building stood empty after having served at some point as the home of Reid Furniture and Appliance Company. With the exception of changes in some of the doorways, little had outwardly changed in the eighty-five years between the two photos.

DeValls Bluff, ca. 1914 and 1995. Many of the turn-of-the-century small-town churches are now gone, hence a visit to DeValls Bluff provided a pleasant surprise when residents looked at the 1914 card and cheerfully directed us to a side street. In some eighty years the local Baptist church has changed hardly at all; an addition on the back and a sign out front for service times seem to be the only obvious alterations. Today the street is paved, but the telephone pole seems to occupy exactly the same spot.

Helena, ca. 1910 and 1994. Helena's Cherry Street has been in the forefront of the state's Main Street Arkansas project, dedicated to preserving and keeping viable the downtown areas of our state. Although much of the street seen here now has empty buildings, unlike the 1910 view, it is largely intact and awaiting future redevelopment. Changes between the two views include the conversion of the building on the right to Helena National Bank, and the removal of two buildings on the opposite corner.

The creation of the Delta Cultural Center in the restored train depot at the southern end of the street and other similar restoration efforts offer hope for keeping the Mississippi River town's Main Street viable and attractive.

Hotel Marianna, Marianna, Ark.

Marianna, ca. 1910 and 1994. The years have not been kind to the Hotel Marianna, as we found upon searching it out. What had once been a three-story, stately columned hotel in the busy heart of the Lee County seat has become a one- story, closed-up shell of a building, with "modern" columns reaching forlornly to the sky.

Clarksville, 1910 and 1995. In an eighty-five-year span the name of this building has changed from the Johnson County Drug Company to Teeter's Drugs, but the building still stands on the corner and still serves the prescription-drug needs of area residents. At some point panels of siding were put on the lower front, and a permanent awning replaced the canvas ones. The adjacent buildings from 1910 are now gone or replaced.

Pine Bluff, 1909 and 1994. The Union Station was completed in 1906 and allowed the many train passengers visiting Pine Bluff to disembark a block off of Main Street, near fine hotels like the Pines and the Jefferson. The 1909 message on the back of this view (opposite) of a group of posing passengers reads, "Pine Bluff has a wondrous future." Unfortunately, such was not the case for passenger rail service, which ended for Pine Bluff in the 1950s. In 1994 the vacant, silent building awaited plans for restoration and a hopefully productive future use.

St. George Hotel, Berryville, Ark.

Berryville, ca. 1905, 1980, and 1995. Although the shell still stands on the Berryville square, the years have seen significant changes in the St. George Hotel. The hotel, located on the town's Courthouse square, dates from the turn of the century. In 1905 the steps led up directly from the sidewalk, past the picket-fenced yard, and up to a rambling porch. The postcard view shows a woman and her buggy posed on the dirt street.

By 1980 the building no longer served as a hotel, but in the interim additional balconies had been built. The yard is filled with an addition housing a shoe store and gas station on ground level; the picket fence of some seventy-five years before is gone. The graceful veranda porch does not appear to have survived the transition.

By 1995 all the balconies were gone, though the top tower had been glassed in during the preceding fifteen years. The hotel's other windows appear to have been boarded over, and no active commerce is seen at the street-level entrance. The building is still standing, but certainly shows the effects of time, improvement, and neglect.

BIBLIOGRAPHY

Adams, Walter M. *A History of North Little Rock: The Unique City.* Little Rock, Ark.: August House Publishers, 1986.
Berry, Evalena. *Sugar Loaf: Springs Heber's Elegant Watering Place.* Conway, Ark.: River Road Press, 1985.
Berry, Fred, and John Novak. *The History of Arkansas.* Little Rock, Ark.: Rose Publishing Company, 1987.
Black, J. Dickson. *History of Benton County 1836–1936.* Little Rock, Ark.: International Graphics Industries, 1975.
Brown, Dee. *The American Spa.* Little Rock, Ark.: Rose Publishing Company, 1982.
Brown, Kent R. *Fayetteville A Pictorial History.* Norfolk, Va.: Donning Company, 1982.
Commemorative History of Hope, Arkansas. Hope, Ark.: Hempstead County Historical Society, 1992.
Deane, Ernie. *Arkansas Place Names.* Branson, Mo.: The Ozark Mountaineer, 1986.
Donovan, Timothy, and Willard Gatewood Jr. *Governors of Arkansas.* Fayetteville, Ark.: University of Arkansas Press, 1981.
DuVall, Leland. *Arkansas: Colony and State.* Little Rock, Ark.: Rose Publishing Company, 1973.
de Man, George E. N. *Helena: The Ridge, The River, The Romance.* Little Rock, Ark.: Pioneer Press, 1978.
Earngey, Bill. *Arkansas Roadsides.* Little Rock, Ark.: August House Publishers, 1987.
Ferguson, Jim G. *Arkansas Handbook.* Little Rock, Ark.: Commissioner Mines, Manufactures and Agriculture, 1924.
Franks, Kenny A., and Paul F. Lambert, *Early Louisiana and Arkansas Oil: A Photographic History 1901–1946.* College Station, Tex.: Texas A & M Press, 1982.
Gill, John Purifoy, and Marjem Jackson Gill. *On the Courthouse Square in Arkansas.* 1980.
Hendrix, Bobbie Lou. *Crater Of Diamonds: Jewel of Arkansas.* Antoine, Ark.: Bobbie Lou Hendrix, 1989.
Herndon, Dallas T. *Centennial History of Arkansas.* Little Rock, Ark.: The S. J. Clarke Publishing Company, 1922.
The Hot Springs of Arkansas. Hot Springs. Ark.: Missouri Pacific Railroad, ca. 1910.
Leslie, James W. *Pine Bluff and Jefferson County A Pictorial History.* Pine Bluff, Ark.: Pine Bluff News, 1981.
Lester, Jim, and Judy Lester. *Greater Little Rock.* Norfolk, Va.: The Donning Company, 1986.
Life in Arkansas: The First 100 Years. Little Rock, Ark.: Arkansas State Society Daughters of the American Revolution, 1985.
Mapes, Ruth B. *The Arkansas Waterway: People, Places, Events in the Valley.* Little Rock, Ark.: University Press, 1972.
McGinnis, A. C. *A History of Independence County Arkansas.* Batesville, Ark.: The Chronicle Independence County Historical Society, 1976.
McInturff, Orville J. *Searcy County, My Dear: A History of Searcy County, Arkansas.* Marshall, Ark.: Marshall Mountain Wave, 1963.

Messick, Mary Ann. *History of Baxter County.* Little Rock, Ark.: International Graphics, 1973.
A New Benedictine Settlement in Arkansas. Subiaco, Ark.: Subiaco Abbey, 1978.
The Roads of Arkansas. Fredericksburg, Tex.: Shearer Publishing, 1990.
Roy, F. Hampton and Charles Witsell Jr. *How We Lived: Little Rock as an American City.* Little Rock, Ark.: August House Publishing Co., 1984.
Ryan, Dorothy. *Picture Postcards in the United States: 1893-1918.* New York: Clarkson N. Potter, 1982.
Satterfield, Archie. *Country Towns of Arkansas.* Castine, Maine: Country Road Press, 1995.
Scully, Francis, M.D. *Hot Springs, Arkansas and Hot Springs National Park.* Little Rock, Ark.: Pioneer Press, 1966.
Snowden, Deanna. *Mississippi County, Arkansas.* Little Rock, Ark.: August House, 1986.
Stinnet, T. M. *Because the Trail Is There.* Little Rock, Ark.: Arrow Printing, 1976.
Stuck, Charles A. *The Story of Craighead County, Arkansas.* Jonesboro, Ark.: Charles A. Stuck, 1960.
Walters, Charles E. *The Streetcars of Fort Smith.* Fort Smith, Ark.: Fort Smith History Society, 1979.
Williams, Fay. *Arkansans of the Years.* Little Rock, Ark.: C.C. Allard & Associates, 1951.

INDEX

Alexander, 397
Alligator Farm, 415, 446–47
Almyra, 199, 200, 203
Antoine Valley and Gurdon and Fort Smith Railroad, 237
Arkadelphia, 8, 10, 231–36
Arkansas Building, 17
Arkansas City, 215
Arkansas Insane Asylum, 9, 366
Arkansas Razorbacks, 235
Arkansas River, 226–27, 302, 306, 386
Arkansas School for the Blind, 355
Arkansas School for the Deaf, 356–57
Arkansaw Drugstore, 146
Arkansaw Store, 42
Arklavista Farm, 307
Army and Navy Hospital, 417, 418, 431
Ashdown, 255
Augusta, 183

Bald Knob, 102
Banks: Bank of Monte Ne, 52; Bank of Mountain View, 97; Van Buren County Bank, 98; Bank of Blytheville, 141–42; Desha Bank, 215; Columbia County Bank, 240; Citizens National Bank of Hope, 247; Bank of Prescott, 269; National Bank of Mena, 280; Union Trust Company, 369; Helena National Bank, 461
Banks, Burton A., 244–45
Batesville, 69, 81–87
Bathhouses: Alhambra, 412; Lamar Bathhouse, 412; Magnesia Bathhouse, 412; Great Northern, 412, 414, 436; Maurice Bathhouse, 412, 417, 419, 422, 442; Horse Shoe Bathhouse, 412, 437; Imperial Bathhouse, 418; Quapaw Bathhouse, 437
Bauxite, 395
Bearden, 276–77
Bearden, John T., 277
Beaver, 61
Beebe, 101
Beebe, Roswell, 101
Benton, 9, 392–94, 396
Benton County Poor Farm, 32
Bentonville, 11, 32–33, 35
Berry, James H., 55
Berryville, 8, 12, 55–56, 468–70
Big Long Lake, 202
Biggers, 152
Bingen, 248
Black River, 107, 110
Blass Department Store, 359, 361
Blytheville, 107, 137, 141, 143
Booneville, 299, 329–330
Bost, Alfred, 252

Boys Industrial School, 358
Brinkley, 155, 160–63
Bryan, William Jennings, 50
Buck Mays General Store, 92
Buerckle, Louis, 191
Buffalo River, 67–68
Buford, 71
Button, Eva, 372
Byrne, Lawrence, 255
Byrnes, A. M., 21

C. M. Wise's Meat Market, 212
Cabot, 103, 408
Cairo Fulton, 408
Calico Rock, 95
Camden, 231, 271–75
Campbell, H. I., 446
Camp Pike, 6, 387–90
Cannon, 43
Carlisle, 406–7
Carpenter, H., 84
Cash, 122
Castleberry, W. M., 78
Cave City, 106
Cave Springs, 43–44
Centerton, 39
Cincinnati, 26
City of Missouri steamboat, 325
Clark, Sloan and Company Drugstore, 236
Clarksville, 334–35
Clifton, Dr. Arthur, 224
Clinton, 98

Clinton, Dewitt, 198
Cockburn, Thomas, 448
Conway, 399, 400
Corning, 106, 110–11
Corruth, Marvell, 178
Cotter, 73
Cotton Belt Lumber Company, 276–77
Cotton Belt Railroad, 211
Craighead County courthouse, 113
Crittenden, Robert, 123
Crooked Creek, 65
Crosby, Cyrus, 75
Cross, Col. David, 125
Crossett, 185, 205

Danville, 336
Dardanelle, 337–38
Delta Cultural Center, 170, 461
De Queen, 231, 285–87
DeValls Bluff, 459
Dewitt, 198
Diaz, 133
Donaghey, Gov. George, 162, 329, 346, 360, 398

Eagle Clothing House for Men, 115–16
El Dorado, 231, 294–97
El Dorado Petroleum Company, 296
Electric Park, 314–15
Elkins, 30
Empire Realty, 296
Esau, 409–10
Essex Park, 414
Eudora, 212
Eureka Springs, 9, 11, 57–61

Evening Shade, 96

Faulkner, Stanford, 398
Fayetteville, 11, 13–21, 69
Fayetteville City Hospital, 20
Fitzgerald, Edward, 317
Florence Sanitarium, 224
Ford, George, 426
Fordyce, 10, 243–45
Forrest City, 155, 179–80
Fort, Lewis B., 253
Fort Roots, 380, 386
Fort Smith, 7, 10, 299, 301–18
Fort Smith and Van Buren Electric Street Railway Light and Power, 302
Fort Smith High School, 308–9
Fourche River Lumber Company, 409–10
Franklin County courthouse, 328
Freemasons, 82, 359
Frisco Railroad, 28, 36, 57, 94, 311, 407

Galloway Women's College, 16
Genoa Colony, 265–66
Gentry, 34–35
Glenwood, 278
Goshen, 31
Gould, Jay, 127, 414, 430
Grand Leader store, 280
Grant, Ulysses S., 401
Gray, Lucian, 59
Graysonia, 237
Green Forest, 53–54
Greenland, 323
Greenwald's Dry Goods and Shoes, 287
Greenwood, 301

Gum Springs, 238

H. D. Williams Cooperage Company, 90
H. V. Beasley Music Store, 259
Habib Etoch's Delicatessen, 177
Hackett, 322
Hackett, Jeremial, 322
Hamburg, 204
Hank B. Hayne steamboat, 272
Happy Hollow Amusement Park, 443, 444
Harris, 204
Harrisburg, 147–49
Harrison, 12, 63–66
Hartford, 321
Harvey, Coin, 11, 50, 52
Hays, George W., 275
Hazen, 158–59, 457
Heber Springs, 69, 74–77
Helena, 7, 164–77, 461
Helena Opera House, 176
Hellwig, F. F., 420
Helm Furniture store, 191
Henderson State University, 232–33
Hendrix, 346
Hewig, Charlotte, 420
Hickory Grove, 322
Hiram, 77
Hollenberg Music Store, 364
Home Accident Insurance Company, 245
Home Shoe and Clothing Company, 243
Hope, 231, 235, 246–47
Horatio, 256
Hotels: Massey Hotel, 33; Elberta Hotel, 34; Kilhburg Hotel, 46;

Mountain View Hotel, 46; Basin Park, 57; Hotel Adrian, 75–76; Park Hotel, 88, 414, 433–34; Ida May Hotel, 152; Hotel Marion (Forrest City), 180; Cone Hotel, 206; Hotel Trulock, 220; Hotel Jefferson, 220–22; Queen Wilhelmina Hotel, 231, 281; Capitol Hotel, 362; Hotel Marion (Little Rock), 362–63; Milwaukee Hotel, 412; Rockafellow Hotel, 412, 414; Majestic Hotel, 412, 414, 427–28; Arlington Hotel, 412–13, 417, 423–26, 443; Colonial Hotel, 414; Eddy Hotel, 414; Goddard Hotel, 414; Moody Hotel, 414; Richmond Hotel, 414; St. Charles Hotel, 414; Waukesha Hotel, 414; Eastman Hotel, 414, 417, 429–31; Knickerbocker Hotel, 432; Hotel Marianna, 463; St. George Hotel, 468
Hot Spring County courthouse, 250
Hot Springs, 1, 411–53, 450
Hoxie, 106, 135–36
Huntsville, 62
Huttig, 298
Huttig, Charles, 298

Illinois River, 47
Imboden, 134
Independent Order of Odd Fellows, 82–83

J. B. Hannah's store, 97
J. M. Smith's furniture and hardware store, 25
Jackson County courthouse, 131
Jasper, 12, 67, 68
Jefferson County courthouse, 219, 225, 227
John Brown University, 46
Johnson County Drug Company, 465
Joiner, 140
Jonesboro, 114–18
Judsonia, 103–5

Kansas City Southern Railroad, 285
Kate Adams steamboat, 167
Keller, Helen, 363
Knights of Pythias, 18
Kocourek and Son Hardware and Furniture Store, 158

La Crone, Robert, 247
La Harpe, Bernard De, 353
Lake Chicot, 213
Lake Village, 213
Leader Department Store, 296
Leola, 402
Leslie, 90–91
Lewisville, 253
Lincoln, 50
Little Red River, 69
Little Rock, 1, 5, 8–9, 10, 87, 155, 345–82
Lonoke, 345, 403, 405
Lowell, 38

M. W. Ware's Dry Goods Store, 228–29

Mackinaw, 254
Magazine, 332
Magnolia, 240–41
Majestic Theater, 370
Malone Theater, 117
Malvern, 231, 249, 252
Mammoth Spring, 79–80
Mansfield, 319–20
Marianna, 156–57
Marion, 123
Marked Tree, 144–46
Marmaduke, 128
Marshall, 5, 92
Marvell, 178
Maysville, 40
McCormick, Samuel, 406
McCrory, 182
McCulloch, Ed, 49
McDaniel's Livery and Feed, 44
McGehee, 215–17
McRae, Thomas C., 270
Mena, 231, 280–81
Miller County courthouse, 258
Mississippi River, 155, 167, 169, 170, 213, 461
Missouri and North Arkansas Railroad, 61, 63
Missouri Pacific Railroad, 216, 289, 382, 384, 411
Monte Ne, 11, 50, 52
Montgomery, Richard, 268
Monticello Motor Club, 218
Montrose, 206
Morrill, E. J. and George, 345
Morrilton, 299, 343
Morris, Ada, 103
Moscow, 228–29
Mound City Paint store, 304
Mount, Joseph, 356

Mount Ida, 268
Mountain Home, 70–71
Mountain View, 97
Mt. Nebo, 339
Murfreesboro, 279

Napoleon, 81
Nashville, 231, 288
Nation, Carrie, 9, 60
Nettleton, 120–21
North Little Rock, 6, 383–90

Oaklawn Park, 414, 449
Oden, 238
Okolona, 239
Oldrieve, Charles, 168
Old State House, 350
Olivetan Benedictine Sisters, 118
O'Reilly, R. M., 411
Osborn, George, 71
Osceola, 137–39
Ostrich Farm, 415
Ottenheimer, Gus, 373
Otwell, 119
Ouachita Baptist College, 8, 234–35, 287
Ouachita River, 231, 251, 272
Ozark Opera House, 18

Palace Theater, 361
Paragould, 126–27
Paramore, J. W., 127
Paris, 331
Parker, Judge Isaac C., 316
Peabody School, 371
Petit Jean Mountain, 299
Pfeifer's Stone Quarry, 87
Piggott, 108–9, 111
Pine Bluff, 185, 219, 227, 467

Pineville, 93
Pinkerton, William, 425
Pinnacle Mountain, 391
Plummerville, 344
Pocahontas, 150–51
Pope, Gov. John, 350
Portland, 214
Prairie Grove, 29
Prescott, 231, 269–70
Pulaski County courthouse, 352

R. H. Wayland and Son Store, 93
Ravenden Springs, 153
Read, O. P., 406
Rector, 6, 112
Reeves, B. W., 293–94
Reeves, Joseph, 274
Rockafellow, Charles, 435
Rockport Bridge, 251
Rogers, 11, 36–37, 50
Roosevelt, Theodore, 363
Root, Elias, 411
Roots, Logan H., 386
Russellville, 340–42

Salem, 78
Saline County courthouse, 392
Searcy, 16, 69, 99–100
Shaver, "Fighting Bob," 380
Sheridan, 345, 401
Shiloh, 22
Shipman Drug Store, 206
Siloam Springs, 11, 48, 49
Singer and Nolan Drugs, 338
Sisters of Charity of Nazareth, 365
Slatington, 267
Smackover, 289–91
Smith Hardware Company, 332

Snodgrass and Bracy's Drug Store, 368
Southern Anthracite Coal Company, 340
Spadra Creek, 335
Sparks, George T., 313
Springdale, 11, 22–24
Spring River, 79, 94
St. Edward's Infirmary, 312–13
St. Francis River, 121, 145, 179, 181
St. Joe, 106
St. Joseph's Orphanage, 378
St. Louis Iron Mountain and Southern Railroad, 136, 170
St. Louis Southwestern Railroad, 276
St. Paul, 12, 62
St. Vincent Infirmary, 365
Star City, 187
State Capitol Building, 87, 101, 346–49
Stranton, Ema, 284
Stuttgart, 185–97
Subiaco, 299, 333
Sudbury, J. G., 141–42
Sulphur Springs, 11, 46
Summers, 27

Teeter's Drugs, 465
Temple B'Nai Israel, 377
Texarkana, 231, 257–63
Tuberculosis Sanitarium, 329

Ulm, 201
Union County courthouse, 292
Union Furniture Store, 385
United Confederate Veterans' Reunion, 379–81

University of Arkansas, 11, 15–16, 21

Van Buren, 302, 324–26

Waldron, 284
Walnut Ridge, 135–36
Ware, M. W., 229
Warren, 207–10
Welch, Dr. Lee, 97
White County courthouse, 99
White River, 61, 69–70, 106, 129–31
William's Bargain Store, 192
Winslow, 28
Wisarkana Lumber Company, 121
Wolf, Artemus, 17
Woodmen of the World, 347
Wynne, 124–25

Y. and M.V. Railway Incline, 169
Yellville, 6, 88–89
Yocum, 41